WE SHOULD ALL BE ZIONISTS

Essays on the Jewish State and the Path to Peace

Dr Einat Wilf

Editor: Samuel Hyde

ISBN-13: 9798846618268
ISBN-10: 1477123456

Cover design by: Art Painter
Library of Congress Control Number: 2018675309
Printed in the United States of America

CONTENTS

Title Page

Copyright

Introduction

The BDS Pound of Flesh and Anti-Zionism   3

Arguing Israel Contra BDS   10

The Antisemitism Mechanism   23

Durban: A Legacy of Destruction   31

Anti-Zionism: The Innocent Sounding Antisemitism   34

How Not to Think About The Conflict   37

Jewish Power and Powerlessness   44

Zionism and Feminism   48

Confident Zionism   57

Introducing Muslim Zionism   59

What Is The Jewish State After 70 Years?   63

Democracy Against All Odds   66

A Day For Atheist Rebels Taking Charge   74

Israel Doesn't Need Liberal Judaism – It Needs Liberalism   75

Israel Doesn't Need Conservative or Reform Judaism   83

Here Is Why So Many Are Outraged By Israel's Nation-State Law   91

We Are Still A Minority In The Region   95

Israeli Arab MK Mansour Abbas Is What Zionism Intended   99

The Fatal Flaw That Doomed The Oslo Accords   109

The Gaza Protests Are About Ending Israel   113

How UNRWA Prevents Gaza Thriving   116

Let's Lay The Myth To Rest: Rabin Would Not Have Brought Peace   123

The Real Killer Of The Two State Solution   126

There Is No Silence To Be Broken On The Occupation   132

Palestinian Refugee 'Return': Critique   138

Constructive Ambiguity Has Not Worked - Peace Needs Constructive Specificity   151

Western States Fail To Understand Palestinian 'Right of Return'   158

Trump's Peace Plan Could Strengthen Arab-Israeli Relations   167

Why Even The Israeli Left Embraced Trump's Peace Plan   170

Biden Just Threw Israeli-Palestinian Peace Under The Bus   173

American Consulate In East Jerusalem Could Preserve A Two-State Solution   176

Israel's Final Border   180

UAE's Olive Branch   185

Arab Success And Normalization   187

Zionism And Anti-Zionism Course Syllabus   192

About The Author   205

Books By This Author   207

INTRODUCTION

This is a transcript of a speech given on April 10, 2022
Transcribed by Jaime Kardontchik

I want to share with you how I began to think about the conflict, my journey, and how I came to the conclusions that I am going to present here. I grew up in Jerusalem. I was part of the Israeli Left - Israel's Peace Camp, and a member of the Israeli Labor Party. As a young adult, I voted for Prime Minister Itzhak Rabin, and later for Prime Minister Ehud Barak. I very much supported the main idea associated with the Israeli Peace Camp; a straightforward idea known as "Land for Peace." This simple equation was that Israel has a path to peace, and the path to peace is based on "Land for Peace" as a formula.

But which land? The land that Israel captured as a result of the 1967 Six-Day war: the Sinai Peninsula in the South, the Golan Heights in the North, and the West Bank and the Gaza Strip in the center. Why was it necessary to come up with this formula? As I am sure you know, after Israel was established, none of Israel's neighbors were willing to make peace with it. All that Israel's neighbors were willing to do was sign ceasefire agreements. So, when people speak of the pre-1967 borders, those were actually ceasefire lines, not borders. The Arab countries surrounding Israel – Lebanon, Syria, Jordan, and Egypt – made it clear that these were ceasefire lines in an ongoing war. The message was that the battle of 1948-1949 was only temporarily over.

After the impressive victory in 1967 and the capture of all these lands, the "land for peace" idea seemed to be a very successful formula. This was the basis for the peace agreement with Egypt, Israel's most prominent foe. Israel signed a peace agreement with Egypt and, in exchange, gave Egypt the Sinai Peninsula, which was more than twice the size of Israel. We can have a fascinating discussion about whether what we have had with Egypt is peace. Still, we officially signed a peace agreement with Egypt and handed over the entirety of the territory of the Sinai Peninsula.

The 1990's were the decade of the "land for peace" formula. This was also the decade of the Rabin and Barak governments. We negotiated with Syria over the Golan Heights, we signed a peace agreement with Jordan, once Jordan gave up its territorial claims to the West Bank, and, of course, the highlight of the 1990's was the Oslo Accords, when Israel negotiated directly with the Palestinian Liberation Organization, with Yasser Arafat, over the future of the West Bank and Gaza.

The 1990's came to a pinnacle in 2000 when Ehud Barak – the head of the Labor party, the head of the Israeli Peace Camp – went to Camp David. Camp David is symbolic: this is where Israel negotiated the peace agreement with Egypt. He goes to Camp David to meet with Arafat and negotiate a final peace agreement over the future of the West Bank and Gaza. When Ehud Barak – who was elected on a platform of making peace based on the "land for peace" formula – went to Camp David, he put forward a far-reaching proposal, something that was not on the table before, certainly not directly with the Palestinians. His proposal addressed everything that Israelis were told are the obstacles to peace and the things the Palestinians wanted.

Israelis were told that the obstacle to peace was the occupation: Palestinians wanted to end the military presence of Israel in the West Bank and Gaza. The proposal was that the Palestinians would have a fully sovereign independent state in the West Bank and Gaza, thereby ending the occupation. Israel was going to retreat; there would not be a military presence. So, ending the occupation was part of the proposal.

What was the other obstacle to peace we were told? Settlements. So, the State of Palestine, the sovereign independent State of Palestine, would have no settlements. Settlements were either to be dismantled or exchanged for equivalent land. The independent sovereign State of Palestine would end the occupation and have no settlements. So, two obstacles were removed.

Then, what were we told? Jerusalem. Jerusalem was going to be divided: the Jewish neighborhoods for Israel, the Arab, secular neighbors for Palestine, and, then, the question of the Old City: the one square kilometer, which I fondly refer to as "insanity central". That one square kilometer was also going to be divided. We sometimes forget how far-reaching the proposal was: the Holy sites within the Old City were going to be divided between Israel and Palestine. We were told Jerusalem is the problem, an obstacle to peace, but that was also taken care of in the proposal. So, check, check, check. All the Palestinians had to do was say "yes", and they would have had an end to the occupation, a sovereign state, no settlements, a capital in East Jerusalem, including Holy sites. What do they do?

They walk away.

OK. You might say walking away is a negotiating tactic. You know, that happens. Fair enough. But Arafat walks away, and eight years later, in 2008, Abu Mazen [Mahmoud Abbas], the heir of Arafat, steps away from a similar proposal by Prime Minister Ehud Olmert. Arafat walks away, and Abu Mazen later walks away to no criticism from their people. If this is the Palestinian aspiration, you would expect, at least, someone to write an op-ed, a small NGO to be established, something saying: "Are you crazy? We could have had everything we wanted. Go back there into the negotiating room and get us our state".

But there were no such voices. I know that sometimes people say: "It's because you cannot criticize in this society, Palestinian society is not democratic." Look at Russia today. People are holding signs and protesting, and the stakes there are much higher. Palestinian society has never been as oppressive as Russia, yet you see protests in Russia. You did not see protests against Arafat walking away among the Palestinians. Arafat and Abu-Mazen walk away with no criticism from their people, meaning they fulfill what their people want by walking away.

What follows is bloody murder. What follows, especially after Arafat walks away, is a three-year campaign named "the second Intifada," a movement of butchery, massacre, and terrorism. Some of you might remember the incinerated buses, entire families blown to bits for having a Seder in a hotel, or from getting pizza in Haifa. And this butchery is taking place in Israel's cities: Tel-Aviv, Haifa, in Be'er Sheva. Not in the settlements. They say: "the problem is the settlements and the occupation in the West Bank." That is not where this campaign of butchery was taking place.

And many Israelis going through that – myself included – are asking a straightforward question. What do the Palestinians want? Because a Palestinian State that ends the occupation, with no settlements and a capital in East Jerusalem, is not what they want. Or, you could say that they want that, but there is something that they want much, much more. There is something they want so much more than they are willing to walk away from that – for that other thing. What is that other thing?

It turns out that the answer was staring us in the face. Palestinians told us all along what they wanted. We did not listen. Or when we did listen, we explained it away. We did not take it seriously. What did the Palestinians want more than a state, more than ending the occupation, more than no settlements, more than Jerusalem? They told us: "From the river to the sea, that is from the Jordan River to the Mediterranean Sea, Palestine will be free.".

The absolute Palestinian top priority, as they themselves claimed, was the establishment of an Arab Palestinian State with no state for the Jewish people within any borders whatsoever. The goal, which to the credit of the Palestinians, they have been pursuing consistently for a century, has not changed. Unfortunately, there has not been a moment when that goal has changed. The means of pursuing that goal have been different.

In our book "The war of return," my co-writer Adi Schwartz and myself focus on one of these means, the so-called "Right of Return," which, if you read the book, is neither a "right" nor by now "return". It is a mechanism established by the Palestinians, following the war of 1948, to ensure that the war never ends and that the concept of a sovereign Jewish state in even part of the land remains unacceptable and, hopefully in their view, something that can be undone. This has been the goal.

When Adi and I were doing our research for the book, we came across a remarkable analysis of the conflict by the British Foreign Minister after World War II, Ernest Bevin. If you know anything about Ernest Bevin, he was no friend to the Jewish people and Zionism. But Ernest Bevin, in explaining to the British Parliament in 1947 why Britain was reneging on the mandate that they received from the League of Nations to establish a Jewish State, basically giving back the mandate to the heir of the League of Nations, the United Nations, he said the following: "His Majesty's government has concluded that the conflict in the land is irreconcilable". He calls it irreconcilable. He goes on to detail, saying that there were two people on the ground, Jews and Arabs. There was no question that two peoples, two nations exist in the land, and they are not religions. Jews and Arabs are two distinct collectives. And he goes on to detail what the top priority is for each of these collectives, for the Jews and the Arabs. He calls this top priority "a point of principle". He says, for the Jews, the point of principle, the top priority, is to establish a State. The Jews want a State. He says, for the Arabs, the top priority, the point of principle, is to prevent the Jews from establishing a state in any part of the land.

Notice how he defines the conflict. This is the best definition of the conflict to the present day and remains the best predictor for the behavior of the two sides from 1947 to the present. He says: 'Look: the Jews want a State. Period. The Arabs want the Jews not to have a State'. Notice that he is not saying that the conflict is 'the Jews want a State, the Arabs want a State, and they cannot agree on the borders, and it is difficult to figure out how to divide the land'. No. He zeroes in on why the conflict is irreconcilable: the Jews want a State, and the Arabs want the Jews not to have a State. This, by definition, is irreconcilable. Everything else you can divide. You can divide the land, divide the resources, and have all kinds of economic and security arrangements. But the one thing that you cannot divide, the one difference that you cannot split, is between the idea that the Jews want a State and the Arabs want the Jews not to have a State. It is as simple as that.

Now, how do we move from here? If this is the essence of the conflict, how does it end?

It ends in one of two ways. Quite simple. Either those who want a Jewish State will forgo that top priority, or those who believe that there should not be a Jewish state within any borders will forgo their top priority. That's it. That is how we get to lasting peace. Either the Jews forgo their desire for a sovereign State, in essence, they say, 'you know, it is not worth it, there are other places to live, we are
outta here," or the Arabs decide that they are willing to let a Jewish State exist, in some borders. Only in one of those two ways does the conflict end. Truly resolved.

Sometimes I say that the conflict is between Jewish Zionism

and Arab anti-Zionism. For the conflict to end, either Jews forgo their Zionism, forgo their desire for a sovereign State, or Arabs forgo their anti-Zionism, forgo their belief that a Jewish State should not exist within any borders whatsoever. That's it. In the absence of one of these two outcomes, the conflict continues. One could argue that the conflict has been a century-long battle of mutual exhaustion, where the Arabs are trying to exhaust the Jews into giving up on their aspirations for a State and for maintaining that State and the Jews are trying to get the Arabs to forgo their aspiration for them not to be a Jewish State. That's it. And we have been engaged for more than a century in this battle of mutual exhaustion.

The reason that this has been going on for a century is that both sides see indications they are winning: Jews look at their achievements, the establishment of their State, their various military victories, the prosperity of the State, the peace agreements, the Abraham Accords (and we will talk about them in a few minutes), and they say: The Arab world is finally coming to terms with the existence of the Jewish State. Hence, we can see the end of the conflict. But the Arabs on the other side see it differently: No, the Jewish State is weak, Jews are arguing, young Jews abroad are renouncing Zionism, more and more Jews are forgoing their aspirations for a Jewish State. The world is calling the Jewish State apartheid. The world is mobilizing to end the Jewish State. We are winning. We only have to exhaust the other side.

This is where we are. This is what brings the conflict to an end. As I said, both sides believe time is on their side. Someone tweeted recently "The Zionist experiment will not last for more than twenty years; it shows its weaknesses and contradictions. It is not going to last." From their perspective, it is an entirely rational worldview. After we published the book, initially in Hebrew, Adi and I had many meetings with Western journalists and diplomats, especially those from countries funding

UNRWA. This agency constantly fuels the Palestinian worldview that Israel is temporary. We keep on telling them: "Look, you think that you are funding social services, but from the Palestinian perspective, every dollar you are giving to UNWRA is a dollar Palestinians believe is a vote of support on behalf of the West, to their belief that Israel is a temporary experiment destined to end in the near future." The Westerners say: "Oh, that can't be. The Palestinians know this is a delusion; they understand that there will not be a return inside the sovereign State of Israel – which is what the Palestinians demand – so, you know, it is not going to happen. It is a delusion".

We always tell them: Give the Palestinians the respect of taking them at their word. From their perspective and understanding of history, they are not delusional. They open a map. They see seven million Jews existing among half a billion Arabs, near one and a half billion Muslims, most of them still hostile to a Jewish State within any borders. They, not irrationally, conclude that time is on their side. This is why the traditional comparison Palestinians make is of Israelis to "colonizers". Israel is like the French in Algeria, like the Crusaders, a state that lasted eighty-eight years, or more if you do not include Jerusalem. Recently they compared us to the Americans in Afghanistan. From their perspective, we are a foreign people, colonizers who came to land to which we had no connection, no historical affinity or cultural reference. To them, we stole the land, took it from people to whom it belonged, and therefore, like all foreigners, we, the Jews in Israel, are destined to leave if we meet enough resistance and violence. This is the dominant narrative, not just among the Palestinians but in the Arab world.

What do we have on our side? Why, by and large, am I more optimistic these days than I have been for quite some time? Because I do see, for the first time ever, the emergence of an alternative worldview regarding Israel's presence in the region.

The peace agreements that Israel made with Egypt and Jordan

did not fundamentally alter the Arab narrative regarding Israel by which Israel is a foreign, colonial, Western outpost in the region which will one day disappear. The so-called peace agreements with Egypt and Jordan were better understood as non-aggression pacts: there were barely any diplomatic relations, no tourism, no economic relations, and no warmth. Egypt and Jordan continued to promote anti-Israel resolutions in international bodies. Egypt remained the number one producer and promoter of Antisemitic content in Arabic. For decades, Israelis were told this is what peace looks like in the Arab world. As long as the conflict with the Palestinians continues, this is the best that Israelis could hope for.

And then came the Abraham Accords with the Gulf states and later with Morocco: the UAE, Bahrain, and Morocco. And those countries went all in. Immediate warm diplomatic relations, tourism, and economic relations. My Twitter feed is full of daily news about new agreements signed between Gulf countries, Morocco and Israel in education, space, and agriculture. They went all in. Within days of signing the Abraham Accords, they also changed their books, which tells you that you change your books after you sign the peace agreement, not before.

And really, everything is in one word: Abraham.

You could not think of a better word to flip the narrative. The current dominant narrative in the Arab world remains still that Israel is a foreign, colonial implant in the region to which it has no connection and, therefore, is a temporary presence that will be ousted with enough resistance, patience, and violence. In that case, there is no better single word to flip this narrative than saying "Abraham". When you say "Abraham," you acknowledge the Jews as kin, you accept the Jews as people with a history in the region, not as foreigners, but as a people who belong, who have deep-seated historical and cultural roots in the region. Their very identity as a people is wrapped up in the Land of Israel. You can convey all of this by saying, "Abraham."

I am under no illusion that this has not become the dominant narrative in the Arab world. But when this becomes the dominant narrative in the Arab world, it does not have to be exclusive, this will be the day that we will have peace. Because that is what the fundamental conflict is about. The actual conflict is not about, and has never been, about occupation or settlements and not even Jerusalem. It has always been about the Arab, and even broadly the Islamic world view that a Jewish State in any borders in the region is an abomination, gross injustice, and something that, therefore, needs to be made to disappear by any means: wars, terrorism, international condemnations, violence, "return."

This is what the conflict is about. And for the first time in the history of the conflict, we finally have a confident Arab and Muslim narrative that says the opposite. After the Abraham Accords were signed, I became part of the Abraham Accords group, and I ended up talking about Zionism to young Emiratis, Bahrainis and Moroccans. In an almost mirror image of what you hear among some young Jews in the West, they said: "We feel we have been lied to about Israel and Zionism, and we want to understand." Following that, I published an op-ed with two young Emiratis, a man, and a woman, that opens with the following line: "We are a proud Muslim, a proud Arab, and we see no contradiction between that and also being Zionist." They said: "We are Zionists," they did not try to avoid that word. They said: "We see no contradiction between the proud Muslim and Arab identity and support for the Jewish people's right to a sovereign state in at least part of their ancient homeland." For the first time, we have a pro-Zionist, pro-Israel, Arab position that recognizes Israel as a country that reflects an indigenous people, a people with a deep historical and cultural connection to the land.

One of the most impressive developments, which helps me make a powerful point, is that as soon as the Gulf countries and Morocco became favorable towards Israel, they also became favorable toward Jews. You know that as a result of the ethnic cleansing of Jews from the Arab world, there are not many Jews in Arab countries, but the UAE, Bahrain, and Morocco are now going out of their way to show how much they want to celebrate Jewish life in their country. And they are not celebrating dead Jews. They are celebrating living Jews. My twitter feed is full of Bahrainis and Emiratis and Moroccans holding celebrations of Jewish holidays with local Jews or Jewish expats. It helps me make the following point:

In the West today, quite a few are trying to claim that anti-Zionism is not against the Jews. As long as the Jews are against Zionism, we love Jews. Anti-Zionism is just an ideology about Israel. Now, I can split those hairs: anti-Zionism does not necessarily have to be anti-Jewish. This is true in theory. Except that in practice, it always is. In short order, every country, society, party, and campus that turned virulently anti-Zionist became hostile to Jewish life. When the Arab world made anti-Zionism a central tenet, it had no Jews within short order. And those are Jews that pre-existed the Arab and Islamic conquest of the 7th century. The Soviet Union, as soon as it became anti-Zionist and made anti-Zionism a central tenet, became a place that was hostile to Jews, and where Jews left as soon as they could. I could go on: Corbyn's Labor Party [in the UK], certainly American campuses.

When you make anti-Zionism a central tenet of who you are as a country, a society, whatever the theory is, you are not a welcoming place for Jews. And now, we are seeing the opposite: we are seeing that when Arab countries are embracing Israel, are embracing Zionism, understanding the historical connections between the Jewish people, the people of Israel, and the Land of Israel, they also become welcoming and warm places for Jewish life. This is a very instructive example of the profound connection between being warm towards Israel and Zionism and welcoming and being warm towards a prosperous Jewish life.

We are still stuck in the middle of this conflict. Fundamentally, it is a straightforward conflict between Jewish Zionism and Arab anti-Zionism. I want this conflict to end not by Jews forgoing their State but by the Arabs forgoing their mobilization against the Jewish State. When that happens, I believe it will be the most straightforward negotiation. We will have a Jewish State living next to an Arab Palestinian State, but not before much of the Arab world, certainly the Palestinians, forgo the notion that having a Jewish State within any borders is some abomination to which they must dedicate their lives to erase. To bring about that eventuality, sooner rather than later, we must make it clear to Palestinians and the Arab world at large that if their goal is "from the River to the Sea," if their goal is no Jewish State in any borders whatsoever, they will not have our sympathy and support. Not that of the West. But, if they finally adopt a path of having an Arab Palestinian State next to Israel rather than instead of Israel, they will find everyone rushing to support them in that constructive cause.

I.   We Should All Be Zionists

THE BDS POUND OF FLESH AND ANTI-ZIONISM

An edited version was published in Tablet Magazine on May 2022

Several years ago, as I was speaking at an AIPAC conference about Israel, Zionism, and the slow rise (at the time) of Anti-Zionism in the West, a couple of concerned parents approached me. They said, "look Einat, we're here, inside the conference, we get what you're talking about, but our kids, who are the ones who should be hearing you, are outside, protesting with 'If Not Now'". This was the first that I heard of the organization, self-described as "a movement of Jews to end Israel's occupation". I saw nothing special about its appeal to young people. I assumed it was merely the way of the world for young people to rebel against their parents, reflecting changing values and circumstances.

These youngsters grew up into a world where the idea that Jewish life is threatened appeared distant, even ridiculous. They only ever knew Jews with real power, such as political power, state power, and military power. They could therefore see no reason why Israel was necessary or relevant to their lives. They could comfortably believe that Jews could thrive by trusting in the kindness of others. It seemed reasonable to them to believe that Jewish priorities should be to care for others and that concern for Jews by Jews as Jews is a cringe inducing sentiment.

Yet, over the years I found that attributing this anti-Israel activism to the vastly different conditions under which the younger generation of Jews, certainly in the US, has come of age, failed to account for the growing virulence of this activism and the ever-growing demands that were made on Jews to join its ranks. Parents were no longer complaining as much that their kids are active in anti-Israel organizations. Perhaps they have come to accept that as a generational reality. Rather they were expressing growing alarm that their kids were being pressured into such positions. They mentioned even that their kids were beginning to select colleges based on whether they would likely be subject to this kind of pressure.

With the signs of distress multiplying, I realized that something far more sinister was at work. Young Jews were once again subjected to the most recent guise of the ancient bullying of Jews to be "less Jewish" - less visibly Jewish, less confidently Jewish - so that they could be accepted, or at least tolerated, by their host society. It is a phenomenon that I have come to name "The Pound of Flesh". Shakespeare had it backwards. Throughout history, it is not the Jews who have demanded to be handed over a gentile pound of flesh. Rather it has been the Jews who were bullied to hand over a pound of flesh, most times metaphorically, but all too often, literally.

When the demand made to Jews to hand over a Pound of Flesh is metaphorical it constitutes a demand to mutilate Jewish identity so that it becomes somewhat more acceptable to those making the demand. Sometimes the mutilation is visual, demanding that Jews be less visibly Jewish in the public sphere from removing Kippas to pendants to IDF t-shirts. Sometimes it involves severing elements of Jewish identity such as denying Jewish solidarity or the interconnection between Judaism and the Land of Israel. Sometimes nothing less than a public ceremony of exorcism and renunciation, where Jews mutilate their identity vocally and in public, is sufficient so that those around them could be assured that the pound of flesh has indeed been paid.

Tom Holland, in his excellent book "Dominion" on how Christianity had made the West, described the ancient underlying vector of this dynamic as the "program for civic self-improvement that aimed at transforming the very essence of Judaism". Holland describes how the Western ideas of enlightenment and human rights still had at their core the now secularized and universalized ancient Christian "dream that Jewish distinctiveness might be subsumed into an identity that the whole world could share – one in which the laws given by

God to mark the Jews out from other peoples would cease to matter". This is a dream, that despite it becoming "garlanded with the high-flown rhetoric of the Enlightenment" Holland explains, "reached all the way back to Paul."

According to Holland, in introducing the idea of the Enlightenment and universal human rights the West "claimed an authority for itself more universal than that of Christianity", but in doing so "only emphasized the degree to which, in the scale of its ambitions and the scope of its pretensions, it was profoundly Christian". Faced with this all-encompassing new-old vision of universal human rights "Jews could either sign up to this radiant vision, or else be banished into storm-swept darkness". Holland adds that "if this seemed to some Jews a very familiar kind of ultimatum, then that was because it was".

The ancient roots of the Pound of Flesh dynamic mean that it is relentless. It always wants more, and more, and more, until there are no more pounds of flesh remaining to hand over. Either Jews are no longer Jews, or they are no longer alive. Throughout history, and especially since the Enlightenment had secularized and universalized the Christian impulse, what Jews have discovered again and again that there was no number of pounds of flesh that is ever sufficient, that would just let them be, other than perhaps the number of pounds that would spell their annihilation. Almost all Jews have been subjected to this relentless "Pound of Flesh" dynamic and will recognize it viscerally. Those who recognize it most, are those who at one point, facing a T intersection, decided to stand firm and reject handing over that one additional pound of flesh.

I experienced that dynamic myself. 25 years ago, as a young adult, I had the confidence that my opinions granted me access to what David Hirsh, in his important book "Contemporary Left Antisemitism", calls "The Community of the Good". I was an Israeli of the political left. I was a member of the Israeli Labor Party. I worked with left's leaders such as Yossi Beilin, the architect of the Oslo Accords, and Nobel Peace Prize Recipient Shimon Peres. I supported a Palestinian state, vehemently opposed the settlements, sought a rapid end to Israel's military occupation of the West Bank and Gaza, and was thrilled when Israel disengaged from the Gaza strip taking out all settlers and soldiers for good.

But… I was still very much a Zionist. *My support for a two-state solution and a Palestinian state emanated from my desire that the other state in the "two-state solution" be the Jewish state of Israel. Yet, several encounters led me to realize that despite my left-wing badges of distinction, the fact that I was an unapologetic Zionist banished me in the eyes of the so called "Community of the Good" to the "storm-swept darkness" known as the fringes of the lunatic right.* I faced a T intersection. I could either hand over another pound of flesh and engage in an exorcism ceremony of renouncing Zionism, or I could step back and refuse to participate. I realized that the demands to comply with the right thinking of the "Community of the Good" would never end, that whatever I gave, there would always be a demand for more.

And so, I stepped back.

In stepping back, I did not change my opinions about the conflict. I continued to support the equal right of the Jewish and Arab collectives to self-determination each in part of the land. Yet, I accepted that these opinions were no longer sufficient to grant me access to the "Community of the Good". So long as I was determined to remain a Zionist (and I was) I would never be considered a "good enough Jew". I would remain on the outside. In the T intersection between renouncing my Zionism or my "good Jew" status, I renounced my status as a "good Jew". I figured, better to be a confident Jew than a good one.

Based on my own experience, I was able to recognize the Pound of Flesh dynamic as it was playing itself out for Jews in American colleges. When I attended college in the US in the mid 1990's, liberal left-wing Jews could comfortably be pro-Israel and even active in AIPAC. With the emergence of J-Street such Jews found it necessary to move there and then to J-Street U. Then I learnt that many of these young Jews found their new home in the newly established "If Not Now" and then in "Jewish Voices for Peace". Finally, I learnt that if a Jewish student did now show herself to be the militant co-chair of "Students for Justice in Palestine" or wrote an op-ed in the Harvard Crimson proudly supporting the Crimson's editorial endorsing the boycott movement against Israel, she was simply not a good enough Jew.

The "Pound of Flesh" dynamic is also expressed in the demand to repeat with enthusiastic Amens any claims made about Israel, regardless of how outlandish. This was the Placard Strategy at work, equating Israel, Zionism and sometimes just the Star of David drawn on placards, with the greatest evil du jure. Zionism equals Racism. Amen. Zionism equals Apartheid. Amen. Zionism equals Nazism. Of-course. Zionism equals genocide. What else? Oh, Zionism now equals White Supremacism. That's a new one, but sure. This progression of anti-Israel activism by young Jews no longer felt like a natural and understandable choice shaped by different generational circumstances, but the outcome of a relentless dynamic of bullying at work.

These past few months as a Visiting Professor at Georgetown University I taught a course titled "Zionism and Anti-Zionism". In the many office-hours spent discussing student life it became apparent that the "Pound of Flesh" dynamic of anti-Zionist activism operated very much like bullying. Like bullying, it preys on weakness and shame – shame in one's full Jewish identity with its calls to Jewish solidarity and connections to a faraway Land of Israel and the state of Israel. The more one feels shame, the more the anti-Zionist bully can extract more pounds of flesh.

The BDS movement has been one of the most effective users of this "Pound of Flesh" dynamic, inviting young Jews to the cause of

"Justice" only to ultimately demand the mutilation of their Jewish identity. BDS has demanded that Jews not only criticize Israeli actions but sever their relations with Israel completely. Not only students on campus, but Jewish organizations have begun to feel this dynamic at work. Just these past few months, the DC chapter of Sunrise, an organization "mobilizing young people to make climate change an urgent priority across America" pulled out of a DC rally to support voting rights because Jewish organizations which were also participating also dared to incidentally support Israel. The organizations they mentioned, the National Council of Jewish Women, the Reform movement's Religious Action Center, and the Jewish Council for Public Affairs, are some of the most progressive organizations of the Jewish community, devoted to numerous causes of justice and equality. That was still not enough. These organizations, by their mere presence were "sullying" a noble cause. Jews were expected to hand over more pounds of flesh as the price of participation.

More recently, Big Duck, a company that helps non-profits with their communications, declined to work with the Hartman Institute over its connection to Israel. This led the Hartman Institute to issue a statement that identified the precise nature and goal of the "Pound of Flesh" dynamic as "a moving of the goalposts on BDS from Israel to North American Jewish organizations". Hartman correctly noted that this "applies a standard on North American Jewish commitments that would exclude the vast majority of the members of our community". A moving of the goalposts is literally how the "Pound of Flesh" dynamic works. Creating standards that make it nearly impossible for Jews to be fully Jewish is the ancient goal.

My choice to step back from the "Pound of Flesh" dynamic of bullying was a personal one. But I have since met many Jews, older and younger, who shared with me their "Pound of Flesh" moments. They told me of their T-intersection moments when they realized that it would never be enough, that the one additional pound of flesh they were demanded to hand over is not going to be the last. They would never be left alone. They told me how they decided to take a step back, realizing they were turning their backs on the "Community of the Good". But they were clear that the price of their release from their bullies was worth it.

Extracting oneself from the "Pound of Flesh" dynamic is not only the right thing to do, but also the key to mental health. One of the best responses from a student to my "Zionism and Anti-Zionism" course was that it was "better than dozens of hours of therapy". Anti-Zionist bullying takes an emotional toll. It is not a matter of intellectual discourse. It operates at the deepest levels of our Jewish being. The only effective response then is to resist it with confidence and pride and thus rob it of its power to prey. It is difficult to bully confident and proud people. If Anti-Zionists are met with Jews who are proud Zionists, who embrace their Jewish identity fully, it is nearly impossible to shame them into handing over another pound of flesh. Faced with pride and confidence, bullies seek other easier targets.

Indeed, as the "Pound of Flesh" dynamic revealed itself to more Jews as the ancient bullying that it was, some Jews responded by openly and proudly declaring themselves Zionist, especially on campus, and especially in progressive spaces. Whether it is Club Z, World Zionist Congress, or Zioness, Zionism has re-emerged in the West, not as a movement to build a state - happily that has already been accomplished - but as a form of confident Judaism. And so today my response to concerned parents and exhausted students is short and simple. The most effective response to bullies is resistance. The best way to extract oneself from "Pound of Flesh" predators is confidence and pride. The best response to Anti-Zionism, in other words, is Zionism.

ARGUING ISRAEL CONTRA BDS

Transcript of a Lecture given to the Academic Engagement Network on May 2017

I want to share with you my reflections on the larger issues of the BDS movement and Israel, and then move to some of the more specific conceptions of how I believe it is best to tell Israel's story, to analyze the conflict, and to argue our case.

For quite some time now, I've asked myself: what is going on? And the question of what is going on has to do with the fact that, as an Israeli who considers herself very much a liberal and comes from the Israeli left, I was trying to understand how it is that those who are supposedly my colleagues, those with whom I supposedly share values, seem to be turning more and more against an idea that I hold dear, which is Zionism. Why is this becoming so much more virulent? In that question also lies the possibility of beginning to ask whether I or anyone else is right in thinking of themselves as a Zionist. If so many people who supposedly think like us on other issues that we care about turn against this issue, then we might begin to wonder, " So, maybe we should turn against this issue as well." *We are also used to thinking that Jews in general are aligned with liberalism, that a liberal order is the best protector of Jewish existence, both individually and collectively. So when those who are considered liberal turn against something that is very Jewish, such as Zionism, questions arise, and we begin to wonder what is going on.*

This also has to do with a bigger kind of observation that I've made for some time: is hatred of the Jews ever about Jews and what they do? When greater and greater segments of society turn against Jews, does this mean that Jews are doing something wrong? There are times we'd like to believe that this is the case, so we say that it is because of the occupation or because we said this or because we did that, because there is a very comforting underlying premise about it. It means that if we change what we

WE SHOULD ALL BE ZIONISTS

do – we end the occupation, we do not enact these laws – then all of this will go away. But I think the answer to whether or not hatred of the Jews has ever been about the Jews is a simple "no."

If we look to history, if we look to the ebb and the fall of hatred of Jews, the hatred has always been there, but sometimes it peaks and sometimes less so. When does it rise? It rises when there is a crisis in the society that is engaged in hating, not when something has changed with those that are being hated.

When I began to see this rising tide of hatred, of virulence, especially the emotion and the violence that came with it, I did not turn my questions to the problem with Israel's policies; we can discuss that, but this is not the issue. Then what is the crisis that is taking place in the larger society and causing it to engage in this obsessive hatred? What is becoming clear is that there is a long-term crisis of liberal or left-wing thought, and maybe also in academia. And *when there is a crisis of certainty, a crisis of identity, when societies don't know who they are, what they stand for, or why they exist, there is no greater comforting certainty than that the Jews are responsible.* When people began to discuss the rise of intolerant liberalism recently, suddenly I said, "Bingo!" because we began to feel, even though, at first, we didn't understand what was going on. Now it's becoming more evident, and more and more people are discussing the larger trends. The battle that we are waging is not specifically on the issue of the legitimacy of Zionism and Israel; it is a far bigger battle.

As much as we as we might all be interested in correcting the world and changing the situation, it is my belief that we should be interested first and foremost in making sure that, as this battle rages on, we are safe. If there is anything that has changed for Jews in the last few decades since the establishment of the State of Israel – which prompted the growing comfort of Jews in the United States and around the world with the idea of Jewish power – it is that, *even though we recognize that growing hatred means that societies are in crisis, we are now less inclined to allow these societies to resolve their issues on our backs*

And we plan either not to be around when they do that or to fight back, and to make sure that, as they resolve their issues, we do not get hurt in the process, first and foremost, physically, but also in all other ways: intellectually, of course, but also in our ability to thrive, to have the jobs we want, to say the things we want, and to prosper. We will defend that as societies are in crisis and we see the corresponding rise in hatred against Jews and Israel.

We need to acknowledge that this crisis is placing tremendous societal pressure, first and foremost, on young people, on students on American campuses, and it is societal pressure to hand over more and more pounds of flesh, to more and more renounce their association with Zionism and with Israel and with almost any notion of proud, powerful Jewish existence. But what these young people are going to discover one day, as all Jews always have, is that it does not matter how many pounds of flesh you give over, or how powerfully you renounce your Zionism by saying, "Look, I'm a good Jew, I'm not like these other Zionists, I hate Israel, I'm fighting against it, Israel is awful." No matter how much you hand over, you will one day discover that it's not enough.

What we need to be fighting for is to change the environment that creates that pressure. What we have heard about [at this conference] are the first battles, and the victories that represent the initial repelling of the attack are critical. We're getting better and better at saying "Stop! No longer, you don't get to invade." But ultimately, that will not be enough.

The oppositional tactics that were described [at this conference] are good, such as going to the academic associations and asking them, "What does this have to do with anthropology or history or languages?" But over time, what we need to do is change the story, change the narrative, because, while those are specific tactics that are very good for winning specific battles, we need something greater.

Here, I will transition to what I think we need to discuss and to argue. We have two key elements. The first, the one that is on the attack or on the offensive, is the one that has to expose the other side, their motivations, their story. And the other element, which I don't want to call defense because it's much more than that, it's a different line of offense, is to tell Israel's story.

First, on the issue of the attack, of exposing the motivations of those who seek to distinguish Israel's Zionism as a unique form of current evil, I want to offer a new idea, a new definition of what it means to be progressive in this context. I propose that being progressive means actually treating Arabs as equals. That means respecting what they say and taking them at their word. I know that there are neologisms now, like "mansplaining," so maybe I'll coin one called "Westsplaining," when the West seeks to explain what Muslims or Arabs are saying to explain it away. If someone Arab or Muslim will say "I want to kill Jews," their interlocutors will say that they are merely expressing pent up rage for years of colonialism. But they're saying "I want to kill you," so let's start by taking them at their word.

I want to offer the idea that being progressive, first and foremost, means looking at individuals, civilizations, and cultures as equals by giving them the respect of actually taking them at their word and not "Westsplaining" away their motivations. What does that mean? It means that when we see across the Arab and Islamic world that fighting words against Zionism – placing blame on all-powerful Jews, or promoting the idea that the Jews do not have equal rights of self-determination – are all acceptable in that society, we need to conclude that this is what those individuals or governments mean. And we must accept that it doesn't mean that doing so somehow paints them as evil or immoral. I genuinely believe that in this conflict there are no good guys and bad guys, moral guys and immoral guys. There are just small guys and big guys, and I'll explain.

Let's imagine for a moment what the conflict looks like from the perspective of the Arab world. The first part of it is that the Arab world is being asked to accept that the Jewish people have come home after 2000 years. Now who does that? Who comes home after 2000 years, rings the doorbell, knocks at the door and says, "Honey, I'm home after 2000 years?" Can we genuinely agree that this would have been a conflict-making situation anywhere in the world? That's the first thing we're asking them to accept.

Now, I certainly believe that Zionism is one of the world's most inspiring stories of a people who rose up to change their destiny of being victims, to change their future, to pick themselves up and do something different, truly inspiring. But I've also learned that in this life there is a very fine line between inspiring and insane. Truly, this is an insane story. Theodore Herzl [the father of modern Zionism] could have told you that this is how Zionism in his time was received. One of my favorite refrains is from when he published his first book, *Der Judenstaat* [The Jewish State]. It was the talk of Vienna, which was a very Jewish city at the time, kind of like New York today. In all the cafes of Vienna they talked about this crazy new book, and the common refrain was: for 2000 years the Jews waited to have their state and it had to happen to me?

So let's start by accepting that it was an insane idea and we're asking the Arab and Muslim world to accept it. By the way it's not just any people who are saying that they are coming home after 2000 years: it's the Jews, and that matters because this is where we need the new kind of progressivism I'm talking about.

Why does it matter that it's the Jews that have come back? We forget that now, in the 21st century, we live in an era when all ideas, ways of living, forms of faith, and lifestyles are equally respected. But if we are to understand what drives this conflict – and this is what I've learned to say to students, this is how I

WE SHOULD ALL BE ZIONISTS

manage to get through to them – I tell them to please leave the 21st century for a moment and put yourself in the mindset of *Game of Thrones*, as the seventh season is about to begin. What is the mantra of *Game of Thrones*? When it's not "Winter is coming," it's "You win or die." It's brutal, but in such a landscape you either win or you don't. Put yourself in that mindset, that there is a new truth, that Christ is the Messiah, or Mohammed is the Final Prophet. And with that truth, which you and your followers claim to be the final, the only truth, you are out there conquering the world.

Now, how tolerant are you going to be of the tiny pesky little people who say, "No, Christ is not the Messiah, he might be a lovely Rabbi, he's not the Messiah. And Mohammed, he's not a prophet, prophecy has been gone from the earth for centuries." If you think that you win or you die and that you have the final truth, how tolerant are you going to be of that kind of attitude? Obviously not a lot. Thus, in both Christian and Islamic civilizations, as you know very well, Jews were accorded, at best, an inferior status. And the inferior status evolved over time to be part of the culture and theology of these civilizations, so that the Jews could only be tolerated as a miserable marginalized minority. Their misery, in fact, became testimony to what happens to people who fight, who don't accept the final truth.

This is, in my belief, a short primer for all of human history. I know it's very non-academic what I'm saying, but these problems began when those who you were used to thinking of as your inferiors suddenly come and have the gall, or the chutzpah, to say they are equal. How well does that go over? In contrast, today, we are somehow conditioned to believe that, yes, when people claim their equality it's just "Come on in!"

I had a short political career, not a very long one, but it was long enough for me to learn one lesson, the only important lesson of politics, I think: it is in the very nature of power that no one, and that means no one, ever gives it up willingly. *If you want power, you claim equality, or you want a different sharing of power structures, then you have to grab it, you have to fight for it, and you will face backlash. That is in the nature of power. And this is what Zionism did to the Arab and Islamic world: it challenged a power structure that had existed for centuries, where Jews had a place, an inferior place.* They were headed to the dustbin of history. Then, suddenly, not only were they appearing with this crazy story that they were coming home after 2000 years, they were also saying they were equal, they were a nation no less proud, no less important, than the great Arab nation, and they were laying claim to land in the midst of the Arab and Muslim world. And they were taking these two things, the crazy story of coming home after 2000 years, a people who were considered inferior, and the claim of equality, and they were doing all of that when they didn't have high population numbers.

When Israel was born, the ratio of Arabs to Jews in the region was 50- to-1. Now it is 60-to-1, so all of Israel's investments in *aliyah* [Jewish emigration to Israel] and fertility and having lots of babies has really not made much of a dent. We would probably have done much better to invest in female education in the Arab world; that would have improved the ratio much more than all our investments in *aliyah* and making babies. There was never a way that Jews could reproduce themselves out of those proportions; they don't have the numbers and they have this crazy story. In that context, o*f course the Arab world is going to say no to Israel. It is entirely rational, it's not about Arabs being evil and Israel being good, it's about Israel being small and the Arab world being big.*

This is the context we need to bring back. The Palestinians are part of the Arab world; they are also part, broadly speaking, of Islamic civilization. Their engagement in the conflict is not that of some helpless victims who are just at the mercy of outside forces. Can we bring back the progressive idea that they are agents that are making conscious decisions with consequences?

That they are informed by their understanding of history and power from the Arab and Palestinian telling of the conflict: that the Jewish power and the sovereign equal Jews in their midst are a temporary aberration? If so, then, the occupation is not the cause of what we are witnessing; it is the outcome. Because at any given moment the Arab Palestinians had a chance to have the dignity of liberty, of sovereignty in a state of their own. But the price of that liberty, the price of that sovereignty would have been to say "yes" to the Jewish presence, to accept it as permanent and legitimate.

At least to date, the choice has been not to say yes, and this is a conscious choice. *If people can make a conscious choice to say, "Better to suffer the daily humiliations of a military occupation than to suffer the far greater humiliation of accepting that aberration, that presence, as legitimate and final," that is a conscious choice of a people who are masters of their narrative, who in their mind are resisting and suffering for something that is honorable.*

Have you ever wondered why the emphasis in the Palestinian narrative is on the word "justice"? Never on the word "peace," never on the word "sovereignty," never on the word "self-determination." It is justice that they seek because, in their minds, the greatest injustice that has been committed is this undoing of an order where the Jews knew their place. That is the injustice; that is what needs to be corrected.

So, when many people hear "justice for Palestine," what does it sound like? It sounds like we want justice for the downtrodden, right? Who doesn't want justice for the downtrodden? But no: *justice for Palestine is a very clear Arab conception that literally means injustice for the Jewish people, and that needs to be exposed.* I believe that it could be easily exposed by using the tools and the language of equality and of equal rights that are supposedly tools only to be used by the other side.

In my engagement with Arabs, with Palestinians, with progressive crowds, I always ask a simple question: *do you accept that the Jewish people, as a people, as a nation, have the equal right, no more or no less, to sovereignty in their land? I have yet to find large numbers of people who will respond with a resounding "yes."* I have found one such person, a Palestinian who literally paid a very high price for his positions. But in Israel, if I argue for the idea that Arab Palestinians have an equal right to sovereignty and self-determination in part of the land, I don't need courage to hold these views; they are shared by many in Israel.

Again, this is not because Israelis are good or moral people, I want to erase that from the record; we're a small country, so we take what we can get, and that's why we say "yes." But from the Palestinian perspective they don't see why they need to say "yes." For someone actually and clearly to say, "yes, I accept that the Jewish people have come home, that they are not foreigners, that they are not colonialists, that they are not the second Crusader states," (which are all various synonyms for saying they are temporary) is a brave act. To say that "the Jews have a right to this land, just as we have a right to this land and therefore, we each need to have less than what we believe is our full right," takes fortitude. A Palestinian who says such things needs to have so much courage he literally risks his life. Nevertheless, *I believe this is the most effective way for us to argue: the idea of the equal right of both collectives as indigenous people to the land.* I am even willing to say, "let's acknowledge the equal right of both peoples to claim all of the land," but then contend that if both sides insist that all of it is theirs, we will be at war forever.

My Palestinian friend once said, "I don't get it, I don't get it, what do you want?" And I remember telling him, "What do you mean, it's very simple: we want you to disappear, and you want us to disappear. Now, instead of discussing what we want, let's discuss what we can have." So this is what we need to ultimately acknowledge: yes, there are big dreams here on both sides, but there has to be an acknowledgment of the equal right of both indigenous collectives to the land and then an agreement about how to share and divide it.

They want you to think of Martin Luther King, Jr. or Mahatma Gandhi, and they want you to put their movement in that box. But there is no necessary connection between whether a cause is honorable and how it is waged. You can have an honorable cause for which a lot of blood is shed and that is fought for violently; many honorable causes have used violence. And you can have a dishonorable cause that is fought for non-violently. Indeed, the choice to engage in nonviolent battle is not because BDS supporters found religion, and not because they converted en masse to pacifism. The movement made this choice merely because all violent ways have failed. *Wars failed and terrorism failed and the Arab boycott failed, so now we have come to a kind of intellectual warfare. The fact that it is waged by non-violent means should not blind anyone for a moment, because the end goal – the eradication of Israel – is very violent.*

How could a goal be violent, but waged by non-violent means? This means that words have consequences. When Israel and Zionism are repeatedly described as all that is evil in our world, I call this the "placard strategy," because you see it in anti-Israel placards in those demonstrations. You've seen those placards, right? What do they say Israel, Zionism, and the Star of David, equal?

On the other side of the equation, it never says Zionism equals the political movement for the liberation of the Jewish people in their ancient homeland. You have yet to see such a placard. Even though the people at this conference are here to fight for Israel, Zionism, and the right of Jews to support Israel, the placard strategy has been so effective that you all know the litany of charges that have been placed against Israel and Zionism: apartheid and racism and colonialism and imperialism and

Nazism and genocide. And these words are chosen not because they reflect reality, but because they all share the fact that they are synonyms for evil.

When you create a global intellectual mindset that says there is a specific evil out there, this is an invitation to violence. Because what we know about human beings is that, unless they are psychopaths, and that's happily the minority, human beings do not engage in violence unless they believe it's for the good. And there is no greater good on this earth than the eradication of evil. So, *in order to prepare the most extreme form of violence, you need to get people to believe that what they are about to accomplish is the most noble cause of all: the eradication of evil. And this is how a non-violent struggle can have a very violent goal. In this way, the story of Zionism has been hijacked, disfigured, trampled upon, and made into something that no serious Zionist would recognize.*

Now, I want to argue why that happened from the intersectional perspective. I want to argue that Zionism is and has the most powerful intersectional message, which is this: Zionism is not just about the Jews and not only for Jews. What, then, does Zionism really say?

First, we must acknowledge that its message is influenced because it is a daughter of the enlightenment, a daughter of modernity. If, in a non- academic sense, you want to divide all of the premodern era from the modern era, it boils down to this element: in pre-modernity, how you were born determined how you would die, and you could not challenge that because it was preordained. This was how society functioned.

But what is modernity? Modernity means that we can challenge that premise, that how we are born is not how we necessarily die. We can change anything, including gender or our financial position, because our destinies are not preordained. This is a modern idea, and Zionism is a daughter of modernity. Zionism is about people, the Jews, acknowledging that they might have been dealt some of the worst cards in history, but that didn't have to be who they were. That didn't have to be the end of the story. Victimhood does not need to be the Jewish destiny, and Jews do not need to passively wait for God or the Messiah to fix things for them. This is why Zionism was a very secular, even militantly atheist, movement at birth. What did it say to the Jewish people? It said: don't wait for the Messiah, don't wait for God, you be your own Messiah, you be the vehicle of your own redemption.

The story of Zionism is about people being the vehicles of their own redemption. It's a remarkably inspiring idea. It's about the fact that Jews could be oppressed, persecuted, marginalized, even much worse, and then could change that destiny.

This is an intersectional story that Jews must share with all marginalized, oppressed people everywhere - that it can be done. But can it be done by relying on the American individualist model, which says, "Stop whining, go and succeed in life because you're facing no barriers"? No, success is about acknowledging the barriers, the biases, the problems, and then taking collective action. Zionism is about saying that it is collective action that changes history. If you want to break down those barriers, you will not do it alone; instead, you can do it as a group.

That is powerful and that is inspiring, so why is Zionism so defamed? Precisely because of that. If people get the idea that they can succeed in changing long established power structures, what will happen in this world? People might get ideas, and that is dangerous.

It is better for powerful people to make sure that Zionism is separated from blacks and feminists and gays because they don't need to see that it's possible, that they can challenge those power structures and change them. And Zionism even has a sequel to share, an intersectional sequel, because what we have to show is that even once we begin to change our destiny, it's not the end of the story. We are constantly facing backlash, because, when you challenge long established power structures, you will have to defend your gains every day. You will never be able to take them for granted. The Herzlian idea that the Jews will have a state and this will cure the world of its anti- Semitism – well, that didn't work out so well. But that is part of the lesson, that, yes, you can change your fate, you can change history, but you will need to defend your gains, and you will face backlash, and the backlash will have many forms, some of them trying to defame the ideology, the revolution, to the point that maybe no one will want to identify with it and thereby it will be rolled back.

That's the story that we need to bring back. And it's a story that allows us to create amazing coalitions and hopefully to break through to those who are saying that we cannot enter the room and, in many ways, perhaps unbeknownst to them, are playing into that backlash.

And I think those are the key elements. They might sound fanciful at this moment, but I believe that, as we move from making small, effective, reactive victories, we need to move to change the story. Because our ability and especially the ability of our young people to thrive, to feel confident, to know that they can live comfortably in an era of Jewish power and not be challenged, depends on the fact that they will understand that we have a different story to tell and that they, even though they live in the 21st century, are subject still to very powerful forces who want the Jews to know what their place in the world should be.

THE ANTISEMITISM MECHANISM

Opening Statement for the Motion Anti-Zionism is Antisemitism at the Intelligence Squared Debate, London July 2019

Reasonable people would probably all agree that antisemitism is bad. They are unlikely to be seduced by it because they know all too well where it can lead: to Auschwitz, the gas chambers and the descent of entire societies into barbaric violence and madness. But this simple observation about reasonable people is true only with respect to antisemitism in its past forms, which are now easily recognizable as such. *The problem is that antisemitism morphs and changes the way it presents itself so that when new forms appear, at the outset, they look nothing like where they ultimately lead.* As a result, most people are capable of acknowledging these new forms as bad only in retrospect and when it is too late to act. But it is possible to recognize new forms of antisemitism in advance, if the mechanism by which antisemitism implants itself into a society is better known.

This is how the mechanism of antisemitism works: it begins by creating a new collective designation for the Jewish people, which distinguishes them from the general population and sets them apart as different in a way which is relevant to each age in which the mechanism occurs. In Christian Europe this group was simply known as Jews. In secular 19th and 20th century Europe, when religious doctrine was mostly left behind, the same group of people became known as Semites (and that designation was never intended for anyone but Jews). In the Soviet Union, which claimed to not notice differences between peoples and religions, and, having just defeated the Nazis, could not afford to be associated with the Nazi version of antisemitism, the same group became designated at once as Zionists and "Rootless Cosmopolitans". And today, in the West, the same group is designated by reference to the Jewish state – as pro-Israel Jews and Zionists. But regardless of how the labels change with the era, the designated group is always the Jews.

The mechanism then operates by projecting onto this designated group the qualities that society finds most loathsome at the specific age and time. These loathsome qualities are described as immutable characteristics essential to the group. Thus, each member of the group is guilty by its very membership in the group and has no way of escaping its collective iniquity – as long as it is in the group. In Christian Europe Jews were all Christ killers and collectively bore that sin. To the Nazis in secular 20th century Europe, the Semites were an impure race. To the Soviets, Zionists were inherent capitalists and imperialists. And today? Israel is described as "born in sin" and Zionists and the State of Israel are the ultimate violators of human rights.

The vilification and resulting subsequent persecution of the designated group is then justified by appealing to the most highly regarded and respected source of authority of the given era. In Christian Europe it was the authority of the religious doctrine of the Church. For secular 19th and 20th century Europe, and ultimately the Nazis, the claimed authority switched to science as the focus on Jews morphed from their religion to their race. Yet continuity with previous Jew hatred was maintained as German theologians claimed that Jesus was an Aryan descended from Galilean gentiles. For the Soviets, the authority was the Communist Party and its doctrine. In our own era, it is international law and human rights. And again, preserving continuity with previous forms of antisemitism, the fact that Jesus was a Jew is again denied and replaced with the a-historical idea of Jesus as a retroactive Palestinian.

The appeal to the power of the highest authority of the era is necessary for the mechanism to work. It bestows the aura of rationality and respectability on the presentation of the Jews or Semites or Zionists as uniquely evil. Without this appeal to authority, which enables the distortion and perversion of observable reality, the vilification of Jews is far harder to justify, and cannot gain broad support, certainly not among the elite of society whose endorsement is necessary.

Thus, it was only by appealing to the authority of Christian religious doctrine that people could be convinced that Jews living in the 12th century were all somehow collectively responsible for the crucifixion of the son of God over a thousand years earlier and were inherently all guilty of that sin. It was only by appealing to the authority of a warped science that the very Jews who had successfully contributed to European society could suddenly be deemed an inherent threat to it due to racial impurity. It was only by appealing to the high authority of Communist doctrine, that the Soviets could convince people that Jews, many of whom were actually the first to support socialism and Communism, could be capitalists set on destroying the system.

And today, nearly eight decades after the Holocaust, when it is socially unacceptable to be overtly or obviously antisemitic, it is by appealing to the authority of human rights that so many in the West have become deeply convinced that Israel, pro-Israel Jews, and Zionists are the greatest violators of the sacred values of human rights. To that end, the context of the Jewish people's existence as a tiny ethnic minority in a region beset by violent inter-religious, ethnic and tribal conflicts is entirely ignored. Israel is placed under an unparalleled microscope, with its every move, especially moves taken for the purpose of self-defense, obsessively analyzed and held to a standard designed to be impossible to attain. In this manner, the Jews again are cast as uniquely evil and a threat to the well-being of humankind.

But why go to all that effort, age after age, society after society, to single out one group of people and project upon it the greatest sin of the day?

The reason is that human beings have a primal need for scapegoats. According to French anthropologist Rene Girard, when societies are in crisis, a psychosocial mechanism of

25

directing communal anger at a single individual or group is activated. This enables the society undergoing the crisis to unite its efforts as people communally project their anger onto a specified enemy, thus avoiding conflict with one another. Girard called this process 'scapegoating', referring to the ancient ritual where communal sins were metaphorically imposed upon a sacrificial goat.

For whatever reason, throughout history and across nations, religions and cultures, the Jewish people have repeatedly been designated scapegoats. While the process of scapegoating might initially help a society maintain its cohesion through crisis, it becomes dangerous and deadly when the scapegoat is identified as the sole obstacle to society's ability to emerge from the crisis – an obstacle which therefore must be removed by whatever means necessary. This is what justifies the persecution, and ultimately even the annihilation, of the Jews – because the process of scapegoating of the Jews creates the false hope that by removing them the crisis would end and a better, safer, more perfect world would be realized.

In this manner, for medieval Christianity, the very continued existence of Jews stood as the obstacle to personal and collective salvation through Christ. For Germans and other Europeans, those of the Semitic race stood between them and the true glory which belonged to the Aryan Race by right. For Stalin, Zionists stood in the way of a Communist utopia. And today, Israel and Zionists somehow stand as the obstacle to justice and peaceful coexistence in the Middle East and even as the sole obstacle to a better world anchored in full respect for human rights.

But unlike ancient animal scapegoats, human scapegoats vigorously resist their sacrifice, and try to organize their fellow humans in that resistance. So the society in need of the human scapegoat must take action to reduce the capacity of their designated human scapegoats to resist. This is accomplished insidiously, as society slowly strips Jews of their defenses. This is most effectively done gradually – nearly imperceptibly, so as to mask the coming danger and prevent Jews from organizing effectively against it.

Antisemitism in Nazi Germany did not start by taking citizenship away from Jews or confiscating their assets and forcing them into ghettos and concentration camps. It started slowly by easing Jews out of the coveted professional positions they had worked so hard to attain, and which gave them a sense of security achieved through several decades of European emancipation. The persecution and oppression of the Jews in the Soviet Union began by removing Jewish scholars from the sciences and other positions of influence. These small, initial steps are easy to downplay, if not ignore entirely, with the assumption that they are temporary, coincidental, and unlikely to have any significant impact on the future of Jews in the society.

Today, American and other Western Jews, now designated as pro-Israel or Zionists, are similarly increasingly finding themselves unwelcome and pushed out of the very spaces they value most in society, the spaces which for decades have given them the greatest sense of security and belonging. For example, Jewish students in the US are beginning to feel unwelcome in elite colleges and universities, which are increasingly known for their virulent anti-Zionism. Liberal and progressive Jews are finding they are not welcome in the progressive circles which have long been their political and social homes. Jews in Britain are finding they can no longer be in the Labor Party, also their traditional political home.

But even when Jews begin to sense the looming danger, the antisemitic mechanism lures them into dropping their own defenses by convincing them that by "opting out" of the collective group designation they will, as individuals, be spared. In Nazi Germany Jews were told initially that if they were the "good kind" of Jew – for example, those who fought for Germany in WWI – they would be spared.

They were not.

Today, in the United States and the West, Jews are being convinced and are convincing themselves that they would be spared if they join in the anti-Israel and anti-Zionist accusations. Even in Israel itself, the mechanism is finding more than a few Jewish adherents advocating that Israeli Jews give up their own defenses, which is the state of Israel itself, in favor of a binational state, which in short order would become an Arab state where Jews are the minority. So called human rights advocates demand to know why Jews cannot simply "co-exist" with the Arabs in a single state where both will supposedly be guaranteed full human rights. They insist on that even in the face of the simple fact that binational states, everywhere and certainly in the Middle East, ultimately inevitably descend into bloody mayhem. They insist on that even though the historic reality is that nowhere in the Arab world have Jews ever been given equal rights as a minority and were in fact violently ethnically cleansed from the entire Arab world when they dared express their expectation of political and collective equality with Arabs. Yet those human rights advocates assure Jews in Israel and pro-Israel Jews in the diaspora that somehow, magically, of all places, this one-state will somehow work in the Middle East. All that is needed for this beautiful utopia to be realized is for the Jews to forgo their bizarre insistence on having their own state where they control their destiny and defenses.

It is therefore no accident that two of the primary targets of the campaign to scapegoat Jews are the two places where Jews have organized most effectively for their defense: The State of Israel, and the pro-Israel lobby in the US.

Those who engage in the scapegoating of Israel and Zionists claim this is all a coincidence. They try to convince the world that the fact that the targets of this latest form of virulent hatred – Jews -

bear a striking resemblance to those who were targets in previous times – also Jews - is sheer coincidence. They will insist that their only complaint against Jews is Israel's alleged human rights violations. They will claim that the fact that the charges against Zionist Jews appear strikingly like variations on the ancient themes of antisemitism – cosmic evil, bloodthirst, conspiracies of money operating behind the scenes - is sheer coincidence. Even as they actively and relentlessly campaign against Israel, many of these scapegoaters will actually claim that they themselves are fighting antisemitism, but it will always be the old, easy to identify kind, that comes from neo-Nazis and right-wing nationalists, which is already commonly acknowledged as bad.

But the truth is that Anti-Zionism is no different than any of the previous iterations of Jew hatred and antisemitism. It is merely the new, shiny, innocent-looking, incarnation.

But if so, why is this scapegoating mechanism activated now?

Historically, rising tides of antisemitism were triggered not by any marked change in the actions of those who were targeted and hated – the Jews, but rather by crises in the societies doing the targeting and hating. It is always in times of crisis that the scapegoating mechanism is activated, and with it the rise of antisemitism.

Thus, it was the threat to the Church hierarchy from the split between Roman Catholicism and Greek Orthodoxy in the 11th century and the successive waves of Muslim conquest which triggered the rise of the virulent antisemitism of medieval Christianity. Another peak was triggered by the **Black Death** plague which swept across Europe in the mid-14th century annihilating more than third of the population, and for which the Jews were blamed. The depth and extent of the economic, financial and social crises of 1920's Germany facilitated the rise of Nazism, and the post war Soviet Union had to contend with the devastation of the Second World War and the stalling of Soviet industrialization.

And humanity today, especially in the West, is yet again in a time of crisis. There is a profound crisis of identity and control, as people are gripped by an anxiety of no longer knowing who they are or what they stand for. Technology questions the very notion of human intelligence and the very idea of humanity. Extreme and changing climate undermines confidence in the future of our species on the planet. Immigration questions group belonging and identity. The persistence of racial and gender inequality undermines notions of progress and our most fundamental values. Politics are polarized, debate has become unhinged and the center can no longer hold. The leaders, or lack thereof leave many feeling there is no steady hand at the helm. Few still look to the future with a sense of hope or security. Old certainties are failing, and none have emerged yet to replace them. And there are few greater certainties in this world than that the Jews are to blame. To alleviate the crisis then, Jews are expected to assume, once again, their role as scapegoats.

And so, the antisemitic mechanism is activated. The Jews are given a collective designation onto which the most loathsome and immutable characteristics, as deemed by the highest and most respected authority, are imputed, and the effort to marginalize them and strip them of their defenses is set in motion. This is done so that when the process is complete, and the scapegoat sacrificed, a better, more humane, more perfect world will emerge.

It never does. *Instead, if the antisemitic mechanism is allowed to reach its full scope, what will happen is that which has happened repeatedly in the past. If Israel is somehow eliminated, and Jews rendered defenseless, the world will look back once more on its actions in horror, hang its head and wring its hands and ask itself how this could have happened, and will vow Never Again. Again.*

DURBAN: A LEGACY OF DESTRUCTION

Essay for The International Legal Forum on the 20th Anniversary of Durban IV, September 2021

In 1991 UN General Assembly Resolution 3379, famously, or infamously, known as Zionism is Racism resolution, was revoked by the United Nations. Whereas the initial resolution was passed by a vote of 72 to 35 with 32 abstentions, the resolution revoking the determination clause that "Zionism is a form of racism and racial discrimination" was passed by a vote of 111 nations, of which 90 sponsored the resolution, to 25 against with 13 abstentions. This overwhelming revocation was considered a long-overdue correction for a resolution that marked a low point in the UN's history and "mocked the pledge and principles upon which the UN was founded", as stated by then US President. But this moment proved fleeting.

When the World Conference Against Racism convened in 2001 under the UN auspices in Durban, South Africa, it found it expedient to revive this equation of Zionism to Racism. Convening in a South Africa where the effects of Apartheid were still very much prevalent and where the system of racist inequality continued to persist in all but name, the members of the conference found it more urgent to fight a non-existent form of racism, rather than the ones that were evident all around them. In doing so, the Durban conference was at once operating against the very principle on which the entire global political system, including the UN, was based, running away from its mandate to fight racism, and making a major contribution to preventing peace.

To equate the movement for the liberation and self-determination of the Jewish people in their homeland to racism and racial discrimination was to undermine the very principle upon which the entire global political system rested since the fall of empires. Throughout the 20th century as nation after nation, peoples after peoples, released themselves from the yoke of empire, establishing their own nation-states, they did so in the name of self- determination of peoples. This became the organizing principle of the global political system, including the UN itself, a body that brings together the sovereign nation-states of self-determining peoples.

To argue that for the Jewish people to pursue self-determination, a respected principle that underpinned the other nation-state members of the UN, is racism, was at best to question the entire principle of self-determination for peoples, or at the very worst, to single out the Jewish people, and only the Jewish people, from ever pursuing this right. In doing so, those who participated in reviving this equation of Zionism to Racism betrayed the very mandate they were given to fight racism by perverting the very notion of racism and engaging in the age-old practice of finding a Jewish scapegoat to avoid dealing with deep and abiding problems at home.

Not content with undermining UN principles and betraying its mandate to fight racism, the Durban conference also made a major contribution to preventing peace. The decade between revoking and reviving "Zionism is Racism" demonstrated the role of vilification of Israel and Zionism in preventing peace. The revocation was part of the Madrid Conference, emphasizing the link between making peace and accepting Israel as a legitimate and even indigenous presence in the region, rather than a foreign implant that must be ousted with violence. This message was heard in Israel and brought about the revival of the Israeli peace camp, the election of a Labor government led by Prime Minister Rabin, the launching of the Oslo Accords, and a series of Israeli retreats from Gaza and the West Bank.

In stark contrast, the revival of the equation at Durban came only a few short months after Yasser Arafat and the Palestinian people violently rejected the boldest and most far-reaching proposal for ending the conflict by establishing a Palestinian state in the West Bank and Gaza, free of settlements, with Jerusalem as its capital, put forth by Ehud Barak, a successor to Rabin.

Rather than sending a message to Palestinians that Jews are a people with a deep connection to the land and that competing claims for the same piece of land are best settled by agreeing that while each side could have some of the land, neither will have it all, in vilifying Zionism the Durban conference turned the conflict into one between good and evil.

Evil must be defeated and eradicated. One does negotiate border and security arrangements with evil. This message was heard in Israel loud and clear. Rather than encouraging Israeli peace-making, many in the international community preferred to sustain Palestinian violence and rejectionism.

Twenty years after convening, the Durban conference could look back on two decades of a successful policy of utter destruction. By vilifying Zionism as racism, the conference succeeded in undermining UN foundational principles, betraying its mandate to fight real racism by engaging in the ancient practice of scapegoating Jews and ensuring that peace is all but impossible. Quite a legacy.

ANTI-ZIONISM: THE INNOCENT SOUNDING ANTISEMITISM

Op-Ed for the British Telegraph, May 2021

All reasonable people agree that **anti-Semitism is bad**, but when they say this they usually refer to anti-Semitism in its past forms, particularly of the 1930s. Anti-Semitism, however, is always evolving: it adopts new language and imagery, often to disguise its real meaning. If one understands the mechanism by which it subtly implants itself into a society, we can identify and expose anti-Semitic meaning even where it has been expertly disguised.

It begins, always, by creating a collective designation for the Jewish people, which distinguishes them from the general population. In Christian Europe, the group was simply known as Jews. In secular 19th and 20th century Europe, the same group became known as Semites (and that designation was never intended for anyone but Jews). In the Soviet Union, which could not afford to be associated with the Nazi version of anti-Semitism, the group became designated at once as Zionists and "rootless cosmopolitans". Today, in the West, the same group is designated as **pro-Israel Jews and Zionists**.

The mechanism then projects onto this designated group the qualities that society finds most loathsome at the specific time. In Christian Europe, Jews collectively bore the sin of killing Christ. For Nazis, the Semites were an impure race. For Soviets, Zionists were capitalists and imperialists. And today, Israel is described as "born in sin" and Zionists and the State of Israel as the ultimate violators of human rights.

The vilification and subsequent persecution is justified by appealing to the respected authority of the given era. In Christian Europe it was the Church. For secular Europe it was "science". For the Soviets it was the Communist Party, and in our own era it is human rights.

The appeal to the power of the highest authority bestows an aura of rationality and respectability on the presentation of Jews or Semites or Zionists as uniquely evil. Today, while it is socially unacceptable to be overtly or obviously anti-Semitic, many in the West are deeply convinced that Israel, pro-Israel Jews, and Zionists are the greatest violators of the sacred values of human rights. Jews again are cast as uniquely evil and a threat to the well-being of humankind.

Yet, when Jews sense the looming danger, the anti-Semitic mechanism lures them into dropping their own defences by convincing them that, by "opting out" of the collective, they will be spared. In Nazi Germany, Jews were told initially that if they were the "good kind" of Jew – for example, those who fought for Germany in World War One – they would be spared. They were not.

Today, in the West, Jews are being told that they will be spared if they join the anti-Zionist accusations. Jews are lured into giving up their own defences, which includes the state of Israel itself, in favour of a binational state, which in short order would become a Palestine "From the River to the Sea" where Jews are the minority.

So-called human rights advocates demand to know why Jews cannot simply "co-exist" with the Arabs even in the face of the simple fact that binational states, everywhere and certainly in the Middle East, ultimately and inevitably descend into bloody mayhem. All that is needed for this beautiful utopia to be realised is for the Jews to forgo their bizarre insistence on having their own state where they control their destiny and defences.

Anti-Zionists try to convince the world that the fact that the targets of this latest form of virulent hatred – Jews – bear a striking resemblance to those who were targets in previous

35

times – also Jews – is sheer coincidence. Also sheer coincidence is that the charges against Zionist Jews appear strikingly like variations on the ancient themes of anti-Semitism – cosmic evil, bloodthirst, conspiracies of money operating behind the scenes.

Even as anti-Zionists relentlessly campaign against Israel, they will claim to fight anti-Semitism. But it will be the old, easy to identify kind, that comes from neo-Nazis and Right-wing nationalists, which is already commonly acknowledged as bad. Anti-Zionism is merely the new, shiny, innocent-looking, incarnation of the ancient Jew hatred, anti-Semitism. And if the anti-Semitic mechanism is allowed to reach its full scope, what will happen is that which has happened repeatedly in the past.

If Israel is somehow eliminated in favour of a "Palestine from the River to the Sea", and Jews rendered defenceless, the world will look back once more on its actions in horror, hang its head and wring its hands and ask itself how this could have happened, and will vow Never Again. Again.

HOW NOT TO THINK ABOUT THE CONFLICT
Essay for Sapir Journal, April 2021

Over a year ago, pre-COVID, when delegations of students were still coming to Israel on planes, I met with a group to discuss Israel, Zionism, and the conflict. During the Q&A session, I was asked by one student to comment on how "colorism" affects the conflict between Jews and Arabs, Israelis and Palestinians. While I had often heard this question framed in the context of racism, it was the first time I was asked about the conflict as one of "colorism." Reflecting on this question, I thought that perhaps it had finally dawned on those studying the conflict that, to the extent race means anything, Jews and Arabs definitely do not constitute two separate "races," so perhaps someone thought variations of skin tone — "color" — would make sense of the conflict in a way that Americans could understand.

Since analyzing the conflict in terms of skin tones made about as much sense as race, and since the talk took place in a hotel meeting room in Jaffa, I simply challenged the young student to go out into the city, where the population is a mix of Arabs and Jews, and, upon her return, tell me whether she could tell Jews apart from Arabs based only on their "color." Even without going outside, she admitted she was not likely to be able to do so. Marshaling all my patience gained from years of having to address false parallels and analogies, I explained that Jews and Arabs, Israelis and Palestinians are engaged in a century-old conflict that rests on issues of nation, religion, theology, tribes, receding empires, carved-out states, history, and geography — all great and relevant lenses from which to analyze it. Race and color are not.

Normally, we expect people to try to understand things that are foreign to them by placing them in familiar frameworks and by drawing parallels with their own situations. Having discussed the conflict over the years with groups from India, China, Japan, Europe, Africa, and Latin America, I was always struck by the parallels they found between, on one hand, the history of the Jews, Zionism, and the conflict and, on the other, their own countries and peoples' histories. Those were always interesting for me to hear, and I considered them an honest effort by people to grapple with a place and a people that were not their own. But unlike these earnest attempts to understand a foreign place and people, some parallels are more ill-intentioned, drawn for the express purpose of intervening in the conflict on behalf of one side, or for reasons that are more about the domestic issues of the people drawing the comparisons than about the conflict itself.

Drawing parallels to cast one side in the conflict as evil and the other as good might have the effect of marshaling support and resources for the side that one favors, but such a strategy is counter-productive, and even just plain stupid, if the goal is actually to engage with the real issues at hand, to solve the conflict and attain peace. "Evil" must always be fought and defeated — so to cast the conflict as a fight between good and evil is effectively to argue that no compromise can be made until the other side disappears or signs an unconditional surrender.

For decades, critics have cast Jews, Israel, and Zionism as the evil side in the conflict through their consistent and persistent employment of the "Placard Strategy": utilizing simple equations such as those that might appear on a placard in an anti-Israel demonstration. On one side of the equation are Israel, Zionism, and images such as the Star of David. The evil *du jour* is the other side, whether it is Imperialism, Colonialism, Racism, Apartheid or — for the truly determined — Genocide and Nazism. Most recently, White Supremacy was added to the list.

The Placard Strategy is so effective that it is employed everywhere and anywhere, from the UN (Zionism = Racism), to the International Criminal Court (Israel = Crimes Against Humanity), to various media and social media, where anti-

Israel speakers invariably manage to respond to any question regarding Israel with the words "Apartheid," "Racist," and "Colonialist," regardless of the question or topic discussed. These words are considered a standard reply to Israelis posting photos of themselves eating ice cream in Tel Aviv.

The Placard Strategy has never been about actual facts and policies. If there was ever a time when it was at least used for purposes that had to do with the conflict itself, that time has passed. Nowadays, the equations and parallels reflect more on the domestic concerns of the protesters than they illuminate any real issues in Israel and the Middle East.

I first saw this phenomenon when visiting Ireland and Northern Ireland several years ago. As I traveled around and met with officials, the analogy emerged: Israel = Protestants / Northern Irish / Britain, and the Palestinians = Irish Catholics. As I visited sites throughout Belfast, the Protestant areas were flying Israeli flags, and the Catholic areas had Palestinian flags, creating an eerie feeling that the Northern Irish conflict, supposedly ended by the Good Friday Agreement of 1998, was still simmering.

It wasn't just the flags: Catholics and Protestants alike described the Israeli–Palestinian conflict with intense emotion, usually coupled with remarkable ignorance. One Sinn Féin member of Parliament even went so far as to accuse Israel of committing genocide — which is when I realized that these emotions had nothing to do with our conflict and everything to do with their own. It was as if, with their struggle officially resolved, the Catholics and Protestants couldn't let go — they needed a new way to channel, experience, and display the full range of intense emotions that had fueled them during their own struggle. But this time, of course, they bore none of the consequences of these feelings and opinions. My colleague Igal Ram once termed this *a "Disneyland of Hate": For those outside the actual Israeli–Palestinian conflict, it was a safe — Disneyland — way of experiencing a roller coaster of intense emotions missing from their dull post-peace lives.* In a world that is actually more peaceful than ever, and where negative, violence-related emotions, such as hatred — and especially hatred of groups and collectives — are less legitimate than ever, the continuing acceptance of hatred for Israel endures. Couching it in terms of the Israeli–Palestinian conflict enabled some Irish Catholics a rare and safe outlet for the open expression of the least legitimate emotion of all, hate, in a world where their own official peace agreement had failed to eliminate intense negative emotions built over decades of conflict.

A visit to South Africa provided me with a similar experience. Especially after the 2010 World Cup, South Africa had successfully rebranded itself as the post-apartheid Rainbow Nation. But the situation on the ground was one where apartheid and its effects continued to exist in practice, if not in name. Challenges of rampant poverty, inequality, illiteracy, and corruption plagued the country. Yet, many of the young people I met seemed possessed by what they viewed as the urgent need to fight "Apartheid Israel."

Noticing once again the intensity of their emotions, I realized that they, too, had bought a ticket to this "Disneyland of Hate." Their parents and grandparents had actually fought apartheid in South Africa, paying a hard price but also experiencing the glory not only of common struggle, but of victory. Life for their children was not so dramatic — their job, instead, was the dull and exhausting work of solving the deep-seated problems that apartheid had created. Continuing the glorious battle — just transposing it onto a faraway land with no regard for the actual situation there — meant they could tap into the glory without experiencing any of the pain.

In the United States, the discussion of the Israeli–Palestinian conflict increasingly resembles this "Disneyland of Hate." If American discussions of the conflict were once focused on the conflict itself and on specific policy proposals designed to advance its resolution, this is clearly no longer the case. Like in Ireland and South Africa, the conflict has become a stand-in for American positions, where self-styled social justice warriors substitute the hard and tedious work of addressing domestic challenges with the vicarious heroism of fighting for the grand ideal of "Palestinian Rights."

America is increasingly removed from its years of glorious global victories and celebrated domestic battles. The last war it won was Cold, and its recent "hot" wars have been a string of sorry messes; even the military-industrial complex has realized that it can sell more weapons by promoting peace. The grand battles for civil rights and liberation have attained so much that the current battles for equity and equality now require a consistent focus on far more tedious issues like infrastructure, health, and education. In the absence of these exciting opportunities to defeat real Nazis in actual wars, or to attain decisive gains for civil rights, those who claim to promote social justice have latched on to the conflict in Israel in a desperate effort to appear, if only to their own in-group, as heroic warriors for "justice." It is as if the conflict serves as a hallucinatory drug for those seeking to escape a dull reality and tedious long-term challenges, allowing them to imagine themselves engaged in a heroic struggle between good and evil, where victories are swift and definitive — to be Captain America and save the day.

And so, in an act of blatant neocolonialism, the American story is viewed as the universal prism through which all societies should be understood and analyzed. Blithely ignorant of the specificity of their own experience, the neocolonialists fit the square peg of the conflict into the round hole of American history. Jews are bizarrely cast as "white," and Zionism as a movement of "white supremacy," while Arabs, who look exactly like Jews (Fauda, anyone?), are cast as "people of color." The Israeli–Palestinian conflict is cast as a mirror of race relations in America, but without the relevant local context of slavery, Jim Crow, or any of the specificities of

Jewish, Arab, or Middle Eastern history.

Since these analogies have nothing to do with Israel and everything to do with projections of domestic issues and animosities, the best response is simply to refuse to give them the respect of treating them as honest arguments and dismiss the pretension that these issues have anything to do with Israel or Zionism. At most, the response should acknowledge and address the underlying domestic issues rather than their anti-Zionist mask.

The irony is that the Israeli–Palestinian conflict doesn't provide much in the way of heroism anymore either. It is one of the least violent conflicts in the world, leading to far fewer violent deaths than most American cities experience each year. The contours of the slow separation between the State of Israel and an emerging Palestinian state are becoming more defined, and Israelis and Palestinians continue their close security cooperation. The growing normalization between Israel and many Arab states points to a regional exhaustion with "the conflict," and a sense that Israel is part and parcel of the Middle East. A dull gray envelops a region that once seemed to promise grand battles between good and evil, black and white, Armageddon and salvation. Yet, in a world where so much is colored in dull gray, the market for black and white is as strong as ever. If actual, real-life Israelis, Arabs, and Palestinians are not going to supply the grand battle for right and wrong, then those who are addicted to this hallucinatory drug will have to invent it.

Yes, there are serious, complicated, and appropriate ways to understand the conflict between Israel, its Arab neighbors, and the Palestinians. None of them includes a grand battle between good and evil. But I can testify that when I sit with audiences and talk about the history of Ottoman decline, or the rise of nation-states to replace receding empires, or the interplay of various imperial and Cold War interests with those of various ethnic and religious groups, the eyes of most people glaze over.

They want to know: Who are the good guys? Who are the bad? Which side should I root for — who is my team?

But Israelis and Palestinians, Jews and Arabs, are not sports teams. They are not stand-ins for good and evil, symbols for the struggles in one's own group much closer to home — they are not a drug for generating intense feelings in a dull reality. Israelis and Palestinians, Jews and Arabs, are real people. They are struggling to resolve centuries-long conflicts, which they are slowly doing. That is a far better use of their time than serving as props and collateral damage in the domestic morality tales of other countries, giving an outlet for people to channel negative emotions with which they should be dealing on their own. Which is why, increasingly, Israelis and even Palestinians watch the intense debates taking place halfway across the world in their name and are left wondering: What does all of this have to do with us?

JEWISH POWER AND POWERLESSNESS

Essay for Jewish Insider, October 2018

Power corrupts. That is an ancient insight. Shared by biblical writers, no less than Greek, Roman, Hindu and Chinese ones. B*ut the insight of Zionism, which perhaps only the Jews, as a literate and continuously powerless people, could contribute, was that powerlessness corrupts no less. Zionism emerged, in no small measure, due to the observation that a people, whose very survival depended on the good will of others (which was generally lacking), is corrupted by the need to ingratiate itself with those in power.* Zionist thinkers observed that the constant need to appease those in power in an effort to prevent them unleashing their wrath against the Jews, has taken a heavy toll on the Jewish soul. Zionism sought to correct this corruption of Jewish existence by making Jews masters of their fate, powerful once again, normalized political actors among the nations.

It has taken several generations, but in that sense, Zionism has been a complete triumph. The current generation growing up in Israel appears entirely disconnected from the experience of powerlessness. It conducts itself with the kind of confidence that would have probably made early Zionist leaders kvetch with pride.

Yet, herein lies the problem. After centuries and nearly millennia of being isolated from the corrupting effects of power, by their forced powerlessness, Jews are now experiencing it in full force. In that sense, Jews have indeed become politically normalized.

For Jews living outside of Israel, and even for many in Israel, this might be too much too soon. Many experience and express deep unease with the speed with which Jews have become normalized. In many ways, this is one of the greatest challenges that present-day Zionism and Israel to Jews. One could even describe it as *the theological challenge of Zionism to Judaism: it demonstrates that when possessing power, Jews are no better (and no worse, it should be emphasized) than all other people with power.*

The idea that Jews are somehow a uniquely moral people, capable of managing power differently that all other members of the human species, should have been summarily dismissed by even a cursory reading of the Hebrew bible. After all, if there is one overarching theme of the Hebrew bible it is that of a people constantly corrupted, despite repeated exhortations by a series of prophets.

Yet, f*or Jews living outside of Israel, it has been a comforting thought to consider themselves heirs to a uniquely moral tradition. Many have conflated powerlessness with morality, forgetting that the supposed moral behavior of Jews over the centuries was the simple outcome of facing none of the moral dilemmas faced by those exercising power.*

This has led some to mistakenly believe that it is Israel that is "ruining" the moral standing of the Jews. Worse, this has led some Jews, still at the margins, to promote Jewish powerlessness once again, in an effort to restore the apparent moral purity of a Jewish powerless existence. A generation that has never known what it is to be truly powerless, a generation that has come to believe that the last, truly unprecedented, five decades of Jewish existence in the US and Canada, during which there was always a sovereign state of Israel, seems to believe it has reached a Jewish "end of history." Some Jews, especially younger ones, have come to take it so much for granted, that they consider the tradeoff of power for moral purity a worthwhile one.

But neither the confidence of Israeli Jews that they have reached an "end of history" of Jewish power nor the American Jewish notion that Jews in American have reached an "end of history" of Jewish integration, equality and comfort don't stand up to scrutiny.

The one incontrovertible fact of Jewish existence, one that

has remained unchanged, is size. Jews are, and always have been, a miniscule people. This has remained unchanged despite substantial procreation efforts. The relative size of the Jewish people is such, that even in the absence of a premediated industrial genocide, we cannot procreate our way out of it.

As a result, the Jewish doctrine, certainly in the modern era, whether in Israel or outside it, has been essentially the same, that of a blowfish. Whether through Nobel prizes, Hollywood movies, technology start-ups and a nuclear arsenal, the Jewish people have been engaged in a sustained effort to make sure that no-one in the world be clued in to the fact that the actual number of Jews in the world is a meager 15 million, give or take. It is the reason that we speak of a Judeo-Christian civilization when we are among Christians, or of a fellow proud ancient civilization when we meet with Hindu and Chinese leaders. We cannot afford to be alone. We must, as a matter of survival, punch way, way above our weight.

The unfortunate reality, as we repeatedly experience in the United Nations, where the nations seem to only be united when it is against Israel, is that our size makes us all too easy to gang up on. Despite decades of Jewish achievement and relative power, our miniscule size means that always lurking underneath is the very distinct possibility that the current realities of relative Jewish power and equality would be reversed.

The current leadership of the Jewish people whether in Israel or in the United States, having still experienced the price of Jewish powerlessness and inequality, while effectively engaging in the blowfish strategy, and enjoying the fruits of the current era of Jewish power, is still very much keenly aware of the actual size of the Jewish people and of how reversible the current reality is.

Unfortunately, this awareness is becoming less typical of the confident generation of young Jews in Israel or of the comfortable generation of young Jews in America. Young Jews in Israel and young Jews in America are both under the illusion that they have been luckily disconnected from Jewish history. This is at the source of their so-called distancing. Young Jews in Israel increasingly seem oblivious to the limits of their power, and young Jews in America seem to question the need for power at all. Both are wrong.

No matter how much actual power Jews in Israel amass, their miniscule size, in the region and otherwise, means that they would be wise to recognize its limits and refrain from pursuing the corrupting territorial and other ambitions that ignore that basic insight. For Jews in America, no matter how comfortable the current reality appears, it would be wise to resist the temptations of moral purity that comes from powerlessness. Power corrupts, but powerlessness corrupts no less. Our survival as a minuscule Jewish people depends on Jews, both in Israel and outside it, heeding both insights of Jewish history, which has very much not come to an end.

ZIONISM AND FEMINISM

Essay for The Journal of Contemporary Antisemitism co-authored with Shany Mor, January 2018

Feminism and Zionism are cut from the same cloth. Both movements emerged from the same intellectual and political origins, they both exhibited similar growth trajectories, becoming two of the most successful revolutions to sweep and survive through the twentieth century, both continue to face ferocious backlash, and both remain vibrant and necessary in the twenty-first century. *Feminism and Zionism are daughters of the Enlightenment. They were born of that intellectual revolution against the inevitability of the human condition as one subject to a hierarchical, divinely ordained order, underpinned by a religious system and elaborate theology. Feminism and Zionism are rebellions against that order.* They are both part of the modern overthrowing of a premodern order in which each living creature, born into a station and role in the superstructure of society, remains in that role, carries it out dutifully, and does not challenge it. Feminism and Zionism are infused with resistance against the pre-Enlightenment idea that how you are born should determine how you die.

Feminism and Zionism are ongoing rebellions against millennia-long power structures that assigned women and Jews a "proper place" in society. For women, it was an order dating back to the beginnings of the agricultural era, that simultaneously enabled and necessitated their control as child-bearing properties. For Jews, it was a theological, and by extension social, assignation of their inferior role by the two civilizations that emerged from Judaic monotheism but also claimed to supersede it: Christianity and Islam. Having made the claim to be the bearer of a new truth in the form of a new testament or a new uncorrupted prophecy, the two civilizations could not but develop an adverse attitude toward those Jews who refused conversion and rejected the claims of both these civilizations to be the better and truer interpretations of the original scriptures. Naturally, Christianity—the more direct descendant of Judaism—was more ferocious in its theological and social loathing to those remaining Jews who still would not accept Christ. But Islam, too, was clear in its theology—as well as legal, social, and symbolic structures—that Jews, even when tolerated, were certainly not, and could not be, the equals of Muslims.

Entire cultural structures—civilizations—were built on the edifice of female and Jewish inferiority—so much so that these themes in their multitude of expressions were transparent to those who were raised into those structures. Themes that emphasized female submission and exalted the limited role assigned to women were reinforced in a myriad of ways from the most minute social norms, to legal structures, to almost every form of cultural output from poetry to painting to children's stories. It was this near endless replication of only one possible model of female human life that created a sense of inevitability. If one is born a woman destined to do one thing—bear children to her master, then one inevitably lives her life and dies a woman having done only this one thing (if she is lucky), and it is by this thing alone that her entire value is judged.

Themes that emphasized the moral failure of the Jew were the staple of Christian and some Muslim cultural creations—from Scriptures to paintings to children's tales to linguistic idioms. Since the continued existence of the Jews implied a rejection of Christianity and Islam, the Jew could not be conceived of as a moral being choosing wisely between good and evil. At best, Jews could be tolerated as relics, headed for the dustbin of history, against the inevitable progress of Christianity and Islam. At worst, their continued existence was an intolerable offense, necessitating the exaction of a price. Most commonly, their inferior status, vulnerability, and persecution served as evidence to the fate that awaits those who persist in their rejection of the true path.

Feminism and Zionism challenged all that. They were both forms of refusal to accept the role that others have assigned to women and Jews. They were forms of self-assertion that cried out: *I refuse to be seen how you wish to see me, I refuse to be that which you want me to be, I am not your inferior, I can be so much more than I am allowed to be, and I insist on being free to explore and make the most of my humanity.*

In that, feminism and Zionism were built on self-definition and human agency. Both these movements could emerge only once the secular and radical idea that human beings, individually and collectively, are masters of their fate was introduced. Once human beings could be conceived of as active agents of historical change rather than passive receivers of divine fate, women and Jews could begin to formulate the notion that even if one might be dealt some of the worst cards in history, and by a whole lot of dealers, it does not mean that there is nothing to be done.

Something could be done, but for feminism and Zionism to challenge power structures that have existed for millennia and have been predicated on women and Jews "knowing their place," they could only do so on the footsteps of the modern political revolutions embodying the ideals of liberty, equality, and group solidarity. True, neither women nor Jews were to be included initially in the ideals of equality, but once the ideal of liberating human beings from submission, the essential equality of human life, and the necessity of group solidarity and mobilization for achieving these goals were introduced, it was impossible to prevent these ideas from being adopted, even by those whom the revolution did not initially expect to include.

Feminism and Zionism arose from anger at this kind of hypocrisy. Feminism and Zionism developed as those claiming to espouse the ideals of equality and liberty and solidarity twisted themselves into ideological and religious knots to justify keeping women and Jews out of this new world. Feminism and Zionism came into their own as the logical trajectory of equality among human beings could not but be extended to those who could also lay legitimate claim to being human beings, even if somewhat different from the mold.

It was the growing ability of women and Jews to lay claim to being human beings worthy of equality and liberty, as well as their ability to mobilize their respective groups to make that claim, that made the success of their revolutions possible. As women became more literate and educated, with direct access to knowledge, it became harder to justify their exclusion from that which was considered worthy only of the formerly exclusively literate—such as the right to vote or to attain higher education. Once women had the right to vote and they became highly educated, it became increasingly harder to exclude them from other areas of life.

For Jews, as the promise of integration and emancipation into European society led them to greater achievements from science to art to literature, their continued exclusion under the guise of the new "scientific" ideology of antisemitism, rather than plain old Christian or Islamic the- ology, became ever less tolerable. As Theodor Herzl and other Jews who initially believed that they were lucky enough to live in an age of progress, equality, and tolerance—a time in which they would no longer be excluded from full participation in the dominant society by virtue of being Jews—came to realize that while Europe spoke of equality it failed to practice it, they realized that their true emancipation and liberation from dependency on others would only be possible when they are truly masters of their fate, collectively governing themselves in a state of their own.

Alas, feminist women and Zionist Jews proved themselves ingrates. The more they attained, the more they wanted. Unable

51

to celebrate what they were given, they exhibited an annoying tendency to not just care about being somewhat better off than before but to actually want true equality. It was a tendency that was often resisted by women and Jews themselves, who feared that the fragile achievements they already had would be endangered by movements that insisted on pressing ever forward. The "problem" with feminism and Zionism was that no matter how successful they were, what achievements they brought about for women and Jews, it never seemed to be enough.

This was especially exasperating to some, given that feminism and Zionism were two of the most successful revolutions to emerge from Enlightenment thinking. What began as insane ideas of a mad few became, over a breathtakingly short time, more broadly accepted. The achievements of both movements in each turn were remarkable and of a nature that only a short while earlier would have been considered unthinkable and impossible. Wherever and whenever feminism and Zionism swept through societies, they turned them upside down and inside out. By changing the very image of what it means to be a woman or what it means to be a Jew, it forced change on societies and civilizations that were predicated on a very specific and limited image of what it meant to be either of those things.

That change was not always welcome. In fact, it was resisted at every turn, often violently, even ferociously. The more power — of various kinds—that was amassed by women and Jews, the more their rise felt like an offense to the "proper order of things." *The challenge of feminism and Zionism to millennia-long power structures was never going to go over unchallenged. It is in the very nature of power that no one, ever, gives it up willingly and easily. If women and Jews seemed unable to know "their proper place" and intent on demanding more, then they must be placed back in "their proper place"—if needed, by force.* Indeed, any Jewish or female aspiration to power was conceived as a "provocation." Those supposed "provocations" became legitimate explanations and exculpations for resisting the liberation of both groups. It has been taken as a given that women and Jews who insist on their equality need to make more allowances for the ability of their opponents to restrain themselves, and if they fail to do so, they are berated.

It is, therefore, no coincidence that wher-ever and whenever women and Jews grew in prominence, their rise was met with increasing violence. The so-called Icelandic paradox of a country where women have the most rights and face the greatest incidents of domestic violence is no paradox at all. The fact that the greatest forms of violence against Jews came against the backdrop of their growing success and prominence is no accident either. Even in the lands of Islam, where Jews historically were better treated than in Christian lands (not a particularly high bar...), "trouble [to the Jews] arose when Jews were seen to be get- ting too much power," writes Bernard Lewis in *The Jews of Islam*.1 Lewis explains that "when a persecution occurred ... the usual argument was that the Jews had violated the pact by overstepping their proper place." Therefore, it is no accident, he argues, that "it is during the 19th and 20th centuries, when the *dhimmis* [protected Jews] were no longer prepared to accept or respect the rules, that the most violent and bloody clashes have occurred."

Direct violence has not been the only method by which the backlash against the aspirations of women and Jews for equality has been implemented. Various insidious ways, mostly transparent to those who grew up under cultural expressions designed to signal the proper place for women and Jews, were employed. Despite the secularization of the Christian world, the moral failure of the Jew remained a central theme of discourse, with only the moral failures themselves changing. It could be capitalism or communism or socialism, colonialism, racism or fascism, but the Jewish challenge to the order of things was presented as something that is deeply immoral. For women, the old ideas about their proper place found new vehicles, whether in the form of "The Beauty Myth" or religious "modesty." And so, entire cultures and civilizations were mobilized to drive a wedge between the "Good Woman" and the "Bad Feminist," between the "Good Jew" and the "Bad Zionist."

The difference between the Good and the Bad? Power. A "Good Woman" does not aspire to power; in fact, she feels uncomfortable with it and would be more than happy to forgo it. A "Good Jew" feels queasy with manifestations of Jewish power, and in the face of raw expressions of it rushes to declare his or her renunciation of Zionism. It is no accident that the forms of female and Jewish expressions that are most mocked, criticized, and denigrated are those that involve the expression of power. Indeed, women and Jews are also denied the right to define the terms of their liberation. Feminists constantly are required to bear the burden of proof that *feminism* is not a term for subjugating men, and Zionists struggle to reclaim the word *Zionism* from those who have tirelessly worked to equate it with all of the world's evils. These means have been employed because if the revolutions of feminism and Zionism are ever to be stalled, and even rolled back, women and Jews must come to feel uneasy with power.

It might be baffling to a twenty-first-century reader as to why movements that sought nothing more than equality should continue to face such ferocious backlash. Equality has come to sound so benign, obvious, a taken- for-granted marker of modern society. But when one understands that true equality leads inexorably to a redistribution of power and resources, then it becomes quite understandable why it is that to "those accustomed to privilege, equality feels a whole lot like discrimination." To those young enough to never have known a world where and when equality was not the norm, it is even more difficult to appreciate the hangover effect of historical power structures. Young men in the West might no longer individually think that women are their inferiors, but they would need to exhibit remarkable blindness to argue that they do not inhabit a world in which the social structures, norms, and cultural output were shaped by this assumption. Young people who have always known only a powerful state of Israel might fail to comprehend how the obsession of large parts of Western and Islamic civilization with Israel is an expression of their inability, still, to come to terms with Jewish power and are therefore prone to confusing cause and effect—thinking that the Western and Islamic obsession with Israel is about what Israel does rather than about what Israel is: an expression of Jewish self-mastery and power.

It is in the nature of feminism and Zionism that their proponents cannot rest until they have reached true equality: until the resources of power are redistributed so that women and Jews are no longer ever in danger of being put "back in their place." This can only be achieved with the transformation of the civil national systems that have determined what that "proper place" is. This is why feminism does not stop with education, voting, reproductive rights, equal pay at work, and safety at work. The more it gains, the more it exposes how entrenched the assumption of female inferiority is in the structures of society and the more it presses onward to dismantle them. This is why Zionism has not ended with the establishment of a state for the Jewish people, because the idea of equal sovereign Jews, governing a share of the Earth's land on their own, continues to be ferociously resisted by the large swaths of the two civilizations that were built on the assumption of Jewish disappearance, often with the declared intention of rolling back that Jewish "transgression" in the form of the State of Israel.

These revolutions cannot stop because it quickly becomes apparent that the rewards for playing by the rules of the established power system, for succumbing to the pressure to be a "good Jew" or a "good woman" are fleeting at best. "Good Jews" and "good women" who publicly renounced their fellow "bad Zionists" and "bad feminists" ultimately never found protection in that position from the violence and backlash inflicted on their group. Women who have abjured liberation or certain aspects of it found themselves no more immune to violence against women than the ones who stood at the forefront of the liberation movement. "Good Jews" who have publicly renounced any group affinity with "bad Zionists" or any of the "bad Jews" of the moment ultimately found that they were no more protected from violence and hatred towards Jews than their fellow Jews. In the lands of Islam, the Jews who suffered most and were the immediate target of violence and persecution were precisely those "good Jews," who should have been protected. Those who were not involved in Zionist undertakings were no more protected from violence, persecution, and expulsion than those who were.

Feminism and Zionism started out as revolutions for changing the fate of women and Jews, but as they grew in power and faced growing backlash, they became revolutions for civilizational transformation. Neither feminism nor Zionism will rest until new civilizations—entire cultural systems—emerge to replace those that were predicated on the assumption of female and Jewish otherness and inferiority. Not until almost all men feel completely at ease with the idea of powerful women and most Westerners and Muslims feel at ease with the idea of powerful Jews could these revolutions call it a day, and neither should they.

CONFIDENT ZIONISM

Short Essay for The New Zionist Congress Journal, September 2021

One of the most encouraging developments of recent years has been the rise of a few distinct and courageous voices of Jews on American campuses openly reclaiming Zionism as their own personal identity. They proudly speak of themselves as Zionists and they use Zion in the names of their organizations. In doing so, they are resisting the pressures placed on many young Jews to make rejection of Zionism a key part of their Jewish identity. In reclaiming Zionism, these young Jews are doing so not as a political movement for the establishment of a state for the Jews – happily that is already taken care of - and not even as a label indicating support for Israel and for the idea of Zionism, even though they do. **Their manner of reclaiming Zionism serves to project a confident and full Jewish identity within the US itself.**

This form of Zionism as confident Judaism reflects a growing understanding among these young Jews that the demand made of so many Jews to prove their bona fides as "good Jews" by demanding that they openly reject Zionism has not been earnest and has not been accompanied by any goodwill. What these young Jews have witnessed is that even when fellow Jews engaged in what are essentially public exorcism ceremonies to discard Zionism - proclaiming their hatred of Israel in anything from op-eds to speeches to ongoing activism – they remained essentially suspect. Something more was always demanded.

Moreover, as new peace agreements between Israel and Arab countries were not celebrated by those claiming to speak in the name of advancing peace in the Middle East, it has also become increasingly evident that the demand to reject Zionism was divorced from any real concern for forging a path to peace between Arabs and Jews in the Middle East, Palestinians and Israelis, if it ever was. This demand was exposed as but a new manifestation of the old demand, made perennially of Jews, to prove themselves to the outside world by engaging in some form of mutilation of their full Jewish identity.

Observing this, a few young Jews realized that true courage lay in resisting this demand for endless self-denial, rather than succumbing to it. Realizing that no amount of ingratiation would ever suffice to the outside world, these young Jews have realized that the most powerful path to saying no is by openly declaring themselves as Zionists. They stand proudly as every possible contemporary synonym for evil is lobbed at them, mostly on social media, but also in person, and they know it for what it is – an ancient pathology incarnated into modern form.

The Jewish people have survived and thrived through individual Jews who knew that the future lay in standing up for their people, rather than selling them out. The new Zionists are the confident Jews we need right now.

INTRODUCING MUSLIM ZIONISM

Op-Ed for the Forward, co-authored with Maryam AlZaabi and Ibrahim Al Rashidi, November 2020

(At the time of publication Emirati Maryam AlZaabi was 19-year-old, a student at Sorbonne University in Abu Dhabi, majoring in History and International relations. Ibrahim Al Rashidi, of Emirati and Lebanese origins, was 20-year-old, living in Brazil and studying geography.)

We are a Jewish Zionist, an Arab Zionist and a Muslim Zionist. *It is time to dispense with the idea that to be a proud Arab and Muslim one must be an anti-Zionist. For too long, anti-Zionism was pursued as an essential element of the correct Arab and Muslim identity. This has not brought the Arab and Islamic world greatness. Quite the contrary: The inculcation and dissemination of anti-Zionism in the Arab and Islamic world has resulted in a massive waste of valuable resources.*

Whether it was in the waging of useless wars against Israel which have resulted in death, suffering and displacement, or in the expulsion of almost all of the nearly million Jews who have lived for over a millennium throughout the Arab and Islamic world, or in the economic boycotts of Israel, nothing good came to the Arab and Islamic world from turning anti-Zionism into a central tenet of the identity of hundreds of millions of people.

Even more than all the wasted human and financial resources and unnecessary suffering, it wasted time. We have all, as peoples and nations, been deprived of so much valuable time that could have otherwise been spent building our countries and societies through mutual respect and cooperation.

After all, what is Zionism? It is the political movement for the liberation and self-determination of the Jewish people in their ancient homeland. It is a movement that asks nothing more and nothing less than that the Jews, as a people, should be able to govern themselves as an equal nation in the only land which ever formed the consistent and core part of their identity as a people and a nation.

There is nothing in Arab history and in Islam that necessitates fierce opposition to this idea.
Arab history and culture have a strong and broad basis. Arab civilization at its height contributed to humanity in math, science, astronomy, philosophy, architecture, art, poetry and literature. *Arab identity can and should stand on its own merits and has no real need to resort to the negation of Jews, their peoplehood and their history, to assert itself. There is simply no negative correlation between being a proud Arab and being a Zionist, believing in the Jewish state's right to exist, thrive and be able to defend itself.*

In fact, it was the choice of Arab leaders, most pronounced under Pan-Arabism, to demonize Zionism as a colonialist movement of foreigners who have come to land which belonged exclusively to Arabs, that led them to expend the valuable resources of their proud nations on trying to oust a people who were not at all foreigners and very much belonged in the region where they were forged as a people and a nation.

Long after the Ottomans, the British and the French Empires left the region, Arab leaders presented themselves as still fighting colonialism in the form of anti-Zionism, desperately denying the age-old connection between the people of Israel and the land of Israel, refusing to realize that Zionism was itself an anti-colonial movement that finally gave a long-suffering indigenous people their place in their ancient home. It only takes a person who studies and acknowledges the Middle East's history to rationally come to the conclusion that Jews, Arabs and other ethnic groups are part of this region and should be living and thriving together. Zionism was never about replacing Arabs but about living with them and next to them as an equal nation and people.

Islam, too, is a broad and varied civilization, that, like Judaism, has many schools and interpretations. Those who claim that Islam mandates the negation of Jews and their hatred as evil do not speak for Islam. There are other strong interpretations of Islam that lead in a different direction. Historically, the golden age of Islamic rule is also the one in which Jews residing in the lands of Islam enjoyed a level of acceptance and tolerance that far surpassed that of Europe's at the time. As some spaces in the West today are being beset by virulent anti-Zionism, it is time again for the Arab and Islamic world to demonstrate that its path to greatness does not entail the negation of the Jews nor their equal right to govern themselves, by themselves as sovereigns in their own state.

The United Arab Emirates, with its high rises, vibrant technological economy, global university campuses, and space programs, symbolizes an Arab future powered by a moderate, tolerant Islam. Good relations with Israel, full normalization, and even open Arab and Islamic support for Zionism is part of that future.

Those who cling to the belief that to be a proud Arab and a proud Muslim one must be an anti-Zionist are depriving themselves of a future that could be bright for all. We have wasted too much time. No more.

II. What Is A Jewish State?

WHAT IS THE JEWISH STATE AFTER 70 YEARS?

Short Essay for Jewish News UK, April 2018

Today we celebrate Israel's 70th birthday. Among all that has been written and said about Israel's myriad successes and future challenges, what has been forgotten is what exactly we should be celebrating and why? In other words, what is the Jewish state after 70 years?

There is no single, official all-encompassing definition of the 'right' way to be Jewish and the 'wrong' way to be Jewish. Herein lies the essence of the Jewish state: the ongoing debate about its very nature.

And this has been the case ever since the days of the First Zionist Congress. Zionism and the state of Israel have always been sites of an ongoing and fierce debate about the very fundamental question of what it means to be the Jewish state.

What makes Israel a democracy is necessity. Israel is a democracy not because it has a beautifully-written constitution that guarantees it. It doesn't. Israel is a democracy not because its founding parents read John Locke or John Stuart Mill. They may have, but they also read Karl Marx and Leon Trotsky.

Israel is a democracy because democracy was the only mechanism that was available to mediate and settle the fierce debates about what it meant to be the Jewish state. Having spent more than 50 years fiercely debating the Zionist project, it was logical, if not very natural, to extend the debate to those groups who became citizens of the state of Israel, regardless of their views.

The state of Israel became a fierce debate over what it means to be the Jewish state, with the debate conducted now not only among Zionist Jews, but expanded to include the views of anti-

Zionist Arabs and anti-Zionist Charedi Jews.

The elected parliament of Israel became a place where those who argued against the very existence of the state, or at the very least made it clear that they could very well do without it, were represented: something which does not exist in any other parliament in the world.

Seventy years after declaring independence, Israel is (by one reckoning) the world's tenth oldest continuous democracy. It had universal suffrage from its first day – yes, Arab citizens too, and it has continued to operate without military coups, civil wars, or suspension of elections to this day, surviving even the assassination of a prime minister.

Its first Parliament sat in 1949 and was empowered by an electorate of all its adult citizens, counted equally. Israel is one of only 20 or so countries (out of 200) that has been rated free by Freedom House in each of its annual reports since the organization started keeping track of democracy around the world nearly half a century ago.

It is precisely this stunning achievement in such difficult conditions that makes Israel's quite imperfect – necessarily imperfect – democracy such a fascinating topic. Anyone interested in democracy as such should be very interested in studying Israel, even if they have no interest in the specific Israeli story, Judaism, Zionism, or the conflict.

Israel is a democracy, but not everyone who participates in the democratic system is a democrat. In fact, many have decidedly undemocratic and certainly illiberal visions for the state and the society.

But since none of the non-democratic and illiberal forces within Israel are capable of imposing their will – as much as they may be very loud – Israel's democracy remains vibrant.

Israel can boast of numerous other achievements in high-tech, agriculture and medicine, but perhaps none compares to sustaining 70 years of fierce debate. And as we look to the future, the fact each of us has the feeling that there are still 'not enough of me and way too much of them', means that we can all agree on one thing – given how each one of us fears that 'the others' might take over, it's far better the debate continues, rather than it be settled.

DEMOCRACY AGAINST ALL ODDS

Essay co-authored with Shany Mor for Horizons, The Center for International Relations and Sustainable Development, June 2018

Seventy years after declaring independence, Israel is (by one reckoning) the world's tenth oldest continuous democracy. It had universal suffrage from its first day – yes, Arab citizens too, and it has continued to operate without military coups, civil wars, or suspension of elections to this day, surviving even the assassination of a prime minister.

Its first Parliament sat in 1949 and was empowered by an electorate of all its adult citizens, counted equally. Israel is one of only 20 or so countries (out of 200) that has been rated free by Freedom House in each of its annual reports since the organization started keeping track of democracy around the world nearly half a century ago.

It is precisely this stunning achievement in such difficult conditions that makes Israel's quite imperfect – necessarily imperfect – democracy such a fascinating topic. Anyone interested in democracy as such should be very interested in studying Israel, even if they have no interest in the specific Israeli story, Judaism, Zionism, or the conflict.

Israel is a democracy, but not everyone who participates in the democratic system is a democrat. In fact, many have decidedly undemocratic and certainly illiberal visions for the state and the society. But since none of the non-democratic and illiberal forces within Israel are capable of imposing their will – as much as they may be very loud – Israel's democracy remains vibrant.

Israel can boast of numerous other achievements in high-tech, agriculture and medicine, but perhaps none compares to sustaining 70 years of fierce debate.

And as we look to the future, the fact each of us has the feeling that there are still 'not enough of me and way too much of them', means that we can all agree on one thing – given how each one of us fears that 'the others' might take over, it's far better the debate continues, rather than it be settled.

The intense debate that was the Zionist Congress became the Parliament of the State of Israel—the Knesset. But the Knesset had a unique mark, which the Zionist Congress did not possess, being a voluntary association: it brought into the debate two groups that became part of the State of Israel very much involuntarily: Arabs and Haredi Jews.

Arabs citizens of the State of Israel were understandably less than excited that they had lost the war against partition and had become citizens of a state they never wanted. Haredi Jews viewed the entire Zionist enterprise as a rebellion against God and Messiah—as indeed it was—and were, at best, deeply ambivalent that it was the godless communists of early Zionism who had brought about the establishment of the third sovereign state of the Jewish people. In fact, had it not been for the Holocaust, the vast majority of them would not have immigrated to the newly established state for the purpose of rebuilding their world of Eastern European Yeshivas, which had been annihilated by Nazi Germany.

Having spent more than 50 years fiercely debating the Zionist project, it was logical, if not very natural, to extend the debate to those groups who became citizens of the State of Israel, regardless of their views. From its onset, the State of Israel became a fierce debate over what it means to be the Jewish state, with the debate conducted now not only among Zionist Jews, but expanded to include the views of anti-Zionist Arabs and anti-Zionist Haredi Jews. The elected parliament of the State of Israel became a place where those who argued against the very existence of the State of Israel, or at the very least made it clear that they could very well do without it, were represented: something which does not exist in any other parliament in the world.

Democracy as Necessity

What makes Israel a democracy is necessity. Israel is a democracy not because it has a beautifully written constitution that guarantees democracy. It doesn't. Israel is a democracy not because its founding parents read John Locke or John Stuart Mill. They may have, but they also read Karl Marx and Leon Trotsky. Israel is a democracy because democracy was the only available mechanism to mediate and settle the fierce debates about what it meant to be the Jewish state.

Perhaps the notion that Israel became a democracy out of necessity sounds less inspiring, as if somehow such a democracy is 'less noble' and 'less worthy,' but over time, *just as having no choice in war has meant that Israel had to win, having no choice but to be a democracy has meant that, over time, Israel has become one of the world's most successful and effective democracies.*

Seventy years after declaring independence, Israel is the world's tenth oldest continuous democracy. It had universal suffrage from its first day—yes, Arab citizens too, and it has continued to operate without military coups, civil wars, emergency governments, suspensions of basic political or civil liberties (no opposition leaders in jail), or cancelling of elections to this day, surviving even the assassination of a prime minister.

Israel was not the only newly independent state to emerge in the aftermath of World War II and to begin its days as a democracy, but it has been the only one to never fall, even temporarily, into some kind of authoritarianism.

Even compared to more established and wealthier democracies, Israel can be proud of the stability and longevity of its democracy. Its first parliament sat in 1949 and was empowered by an electorate of all its adult citizens counted equally. The first Belgian Parliament to count women's votes equally was only convened later that same year; the first British Parliament to be elected without the practice of 'plural voting' was elected the following year, in 1950. The final restrictions on women's voting in Switzerland were revoked only in 1990. The vote was only guaranteed for African Americans in the United States in 1965; restrictions on the voting rights of aboriginals in Australia were lifted in 1962; restrictions on the voting rights of first peoples in Canada were definitively lifted in 1960.

Israel is one of only 20 or so countries (out of 200) that has been rated *free* by Freedom House in each of its annual reports since the organization started keeping track of democracy around the world nearly half a century ago. Of the very few countries that have been practicing democracy uninterrupted longer than Israel, most have only done so for slightly longer than Israel (Denmark, Netherlands, Norway, Sweden), and none have done so in conditions of ongoing conflict, repeated wars on multiple fronts, terrorism, waves of immigration in unparalleled proportions, and a population of vast linguistic, national, religious, and ethnic diversity.

It is precisely this stunning achievement under such difficult conditions that makes Israel's quite imperfect—necessarily imperfect—democracy such a fascinating topic of study. In fact, anyone interested in democracy *per se* should be very interested in studying Israel, even if they have no interest in the specific Israeli story, Judaism, Zionism, or the conflict.

So, Israel is very much a democracy. But that does not mean that everyone who participates in the democratic system is a democrat. In fact, many have decidedly undemocratic and certainly illiberal visions for the state and society. But since none of the non-democratic and illiberal forces within Israel are capable of imposing their will—as loud as they may be—Israel's democracy remains vibrant. This is why the system should not be changed.

In Israel, the greater the debate, the stronger the democracy.

As much as Israelis might crave consensus, it is in periods of greater consensus that Israeli democracy has been weakened, and in periods of great strife that Israeli democracy has shown itself to be vibrant. This is the paradox of Israeli democracy; it is more democratic, more open, more inclusive, and more liberal than at any point in its history, but there is greater voice and representation for illiberal, religious, and supremacist worldviews that were once suppressed in the debate.

Democracy and the Territories

All of this is true for the sovereign State of Israel, within what is known as the pre-1967 lines, or, more accurately, as the 1949 armistice lines. Those are the lines that separate the State of Israel from the territories acquired in the 1967 Six-Day War. Initially, all of these territories, tripling Israel's pre-1967 size, came under military occupation.

There is a common mistake and misperception that occupation of territory is illegal. One is often likely to hear that "the Israeli occupation is illegal." Military occupation of territory acquired in war is actually legal, sanctioned by international law in both The Hague Convention of 1907 and the Fourth Geneva Convention of 1949. Both these documents specify the responsibility of occupying powers, but the occupation itself is legal.

The underlying assumption of the legality of occupations, and the reason that, as such, they do not challenge the democratic nature of the occupying power—such that it is—is that they are temporary. That is, the occupying power holds on to the territory until conditions enable the attainment of peace or an end to hostility. For example, the American occupation of parts of Germany ended officially in 1990, and no one has ever challenged America's democracy on those grounds.

Ever since 1967, Israel has indeed demonstrated that it views the occupation of the various post-1967 territories as temporary, and when it did have claims on the territory, it annexed in a way commensurate with its democracy as demonstrated in the following instances:

One, the Sinai Peninsula was handed over to Egypt as part of the 1979 peace agreement. Two, the sparsely populated Golan Heights has been annexed to Israel, with all residents wishing to do so becoming citizens of the State of Israel. With regard to the few who have chosen not to attain citizenship, the reason comes down to the fear that, should the Golan Heights be handed over to Syria, the fact that they have assumed Israeli citizenship will be viewed as a dangerous form of collaboration with the enemy. The possibility of trading the Golan Heights for peace with Syria has been repeatedly pursued by successive Israeli governments, but with the situation in Syria as it is, it is highly likely that the Golan Heights will remain part of Israel and its democracy for the foreseeable future.

Three, the Gaza Strip, under Egyptian military occupation until 1967, was under Israeli occupation between 1967 and 1994, when 80 percent of the Strip was handed over to Palestinian control, as part of an international agreement. In 2005, Israel disengaged from the remainder of the territory and made a full military and civilian retreat from every square kilometer of the area. Israel makes no territorial claims on Gaza, and, despite ongoing military hostilities, Gaza is not part of Israel. Israel is a democracy in an ongoing state of war with Gaza, but the war itself does not challenge Israel's status as a democracy beyond the line that separates Gaza from Israel.

Four, within the West Bank, Israel has annexed some of the territory to form the greater city of Jerusalem. The residents in the annexed territories have the option of becoming citizens of Israel's democracy—an option that the vast majority have rejected, with the view that it is a form of collaboration with the enemy.

Five, the remaining territory of the West Bank was not annexed to Israel. While Israel does argue that it has legitimate claims to at least part of the territory, and while there are those in Israel who demand that Israel annex large parts of it, the State of Israel has not annexed the West Bank. Moreover, Israel has, under successive governments, signalled its willingness to end the military occupation in a peace agreement with the Palestinians. This led to the Oslo Accords (1993), which today governs the lives of the vast majority of Palestinians, as a form of basic self-governance.

Getting to Finality?

In one form or another, Israel has divested itself from most of the territories it acquired by way of its stunning victory over three Arab armies in the Six-Day War. Israel has repeatedly demonstrated that it views the occupation of those territories as temporary and has acted in accordance with that assumption. When it did not, it annexed certain territories and brought their citizens into Israel's democracy. As a result, ***the status of most of the territories has been settled in a way that does not challenge Israeli democracy,*** and as a result Israel is in a gradual process of settling its final borders, as more and more of its Arab enemies are coming to terms with its existence.

The last remaining debate rages over Israel's eastern border and the status of the West Bank. The reason this debate still rages is that, despite bold attempts by Israel in 2000 and 2008 to end the occupation of the West Bank in a full peace agreement with the Palestinians that would have settled all claims, a Palestinian *'yes'* has not been forthcoming.

As a result, there are illiberal, messianic, and supremacist voices, represented in Israel's parliament, that propose a vision of Israeli permanent control over the territory, and one that would deny its Palestinian residents full rights. Should they succeed—which, contrary to the sharp debate, they are a long way from achieving—it would indeed mean that Israel is no longer a full democracy of all of its citizens.

The Israeli parliament is the most diverse workplace in Israel. Every one of the 120 members of the Knesset must contend daily with acknowledging that those whom he or she believes are leading the country on the road to hell have an equal vote and an equal say in shaping the future of the country. Israel's democracy forces us all to realize that the right of all participants to shape the future is equal to one's own—even though what we would really like is for them to disappear.

Israel can boast of numerous achievements, but perhaps none compares to sustaining 70 years of fierce debate. And, as we look to the future, the fact that each of us has the feeling that there are still "not enough of me and way too much of them" means that we can all agree on one thing—given how each one of us fears that 'the others' might take over, it is far better for the debate to continue than for it to be settled.

A DAY FOR ATHEIST REBELS TAKING CHARGE

Short Essay for Forward ahead of Israel's Independence Day, April 2018

Israel's Independence Day is the one day in the Hebrew calendar which truly belongs to the atheist rebels who founded Zionism and brought about the establishment of the State of Israel.

When the modern state of Israel was established, it set the Hebrew calendar as its official state calendar. Given that the Hebrew calendar was mostly the agricultural calendar of the Israelites, it made much more sense in the geographical climate of modern Israel than it ever did in Poland, where Jews kept it religiously as the calendar of a people in exile.

So, when that calendar was reinstated as the official calendar of the modern state of Israel, the ancient, religious holidays were given a new, secular interpretation. Either the national aspect was emphasized, as in the case of Hanukkah, Purim and Passover, or the holidays were reframed as agricultural celebrations of a people in their land, as in the case of **Rosh Hashanah** and Shavuot.

But one day needed no such reframing and reinterpretation, as it was the one day of celebration added to the calendar (the other two were of mourning): the modern Israel's Day of Independence, the day that it declared itself a state and the Jewish people became masters of their fate.

ISRAEL DOESN'T NEED LIBERAL JUDAISM – IT NEEDS LIBERALISM

Op-Ed Co-Authored with Ram Vromen for Forward, October 2018

Several years ago, I (Einat) had the honor of speaking at a Conservative Synagogue in NYC. I was asked why, as a proud Israeli feminist, I am not mobilized for the cause of the Women of the Wall. I admitted that while I am a feminist I am also a devout Atheist, and the importance of praying to a god who does not exist next to the ruins of an outer support wall was entirely alien to me.

The members of the congregation were visibly shocked by my response. And I was shocked that they were shocked. But our mutual astonishment actually clarified something for me: Liberal seemed to have no idea that the people in Israel push for religious pluralism in Israel by focusing on religion — rather than on pluralism — they are actually shooting themselves in the foot. For in so doing, they are seeking a coalition with the very people — religious Israelis — who will never accept them.

In fact, these accusations are nothing new; for years, American Jews have argued that the "State of the Jews" is not truly a home to all Jews, lacking the religious pluralism they find in the Diaspora. And yet, most Israeli Jews have no idea what they're talking about.

As far as Israelis are concerned, they have an incredibly pluralistic society reflecting multiple religious practices, sects, sub-sects and ethnicities. Israeli Jews are remarkably tolerant of a host of different modes of practical ritualistic expression. One can be a devout atheist-shrimp-eating-Shabbat-driving Jew or a fanatical, carry-out-all-the-Mitzvahs one, and all are citizens of the Jewish state.

As a society, Israelis really could care less how citizens express their religious identity, Jewish or otherwise. Of course, this is not what liberal American Jews want when they ask for more "pluralism."

What they mean is having equal standing in the public and political sphere for Conservative and Reform Judaism, which are all but foreign concepts to Israelis.

This distinction is based on a rather fundamental difference in the historical development of Judaism in the US and Israel. It was a colleague at the Jewish People Policy Institute, Prof. Shlomo Fisher, who elucidated this phenomenon for us in his superb essay "American Jews are Protestants, Israeli Jews are Catholics."

There Fisher explains that the liberal Jewish American conception of religion developed in a uniquely American context, where religion is viewed as a personal choice and a form of individual self-expression, officially separate from the political sphere. For American Jews as for Americans more generally, religion is compatible with "pluralism, civil rights and democracy."

Meanwhile, Israelis, following the European model, came to view democracy, civil liberties or pluralism as requiring the overthrow of religion. As opposed to American Jews, for Israelis "religious identity is not really a matter of individual choice or conviction, rather, it goes along with one's national, ethnic or political identity," writes Fisher. In Israel, Jewishness is not an individual choice but part and parcel of the public, political sphere.

It wasn't always so. In the early years of the state of Israel, the cultural elite was secular, even militantly atheist. Under the mistaken assumption that Zionism had completed the reform of Judaism, the question of religion in the public sphere was viewed as the purview of small marginal groups, which would quickly be swept by the forward march of history into secularism.

Unfortunately, Ben Gurion was wrong to think that religion would evaporate. These days, the secular Zionist labor party has ceded power to a coalition of religious nationalists, ultra-religious Haredim, and religious traditionalists. As a result, Judaism itself moved from the margin to the center, becoming a key factor, perhaps *the* key factor, in Israeli politics.

This was a key insight employed by Netanyahu in the 1996 elections — that attitudes towards Jewish religious practice were the single greatest determinant of one's political leaning. He has ridden that insight to the polls again and again, allowing Jewish religion to become the means through which retrograde ideas, illiberal values and increasingly supremacist ideologies promote and cement inequality between Jews and non-Jews, and between men and women. The universal idea that religious "sensitivities" are somehow sacrosanct has lead them to be used to impose increasingly stringent forms of segregation against women.

The Jewish religious male is posited as the superior being for whom all allowances must be made. Under the guise that religious men somehow are deeply offended by the presence of women in the public sphere, women have been pushed to the back of some buses that go through religious neighborhoods, prevented from serving in several roles in the military, and increasingly forced to follow "modesty codes" so as not to "offend" religious male soldiers. Religious arguments also underpin opposition to full LGBTQ equality, and in general oppose any kind of family form that is not Jewish male, Jewish female, Jewish children.

Liberal American Jews, accustomed to the American tradition of religion in the service of liberal values and progress, have observed these developments with dismay and incomprehension and perhaps even denial. They believe that the Jewish religion could play a different role in Israel. They are wrong.

An American philanthropist recently shared with Ram his frustration at the fact that whenever and wherever he sees something wrong in Israel — in the treatment of women, of non-Jews, and expressions of racism and hatred — he also sees a Rabbi. This is not a coincidence. This is not an aberration. This is the role of Jewish religion in Israel.

If American Jews are ever to find a home for their brand of Judaism in Israel, their goal cannot be support for a "kinder, gentler" type of Jewish religion in the public and political sphere, commensurate with their liberal values. Their goal should be no religion at all.

What American Jews Get Wrong About Israeli Liberalism

Liberal American Jews will only be effective in securing a home in Israel for their brand of Jewish practice if their goal is to secure the Zionist project of a national *secular* Jewish existence.

Unlike in America, in Israel, liberal values can *only* be promoted in the context of secularism. As a broad rule (there are individual exceptions of course), the more secular Israelis will uphold liberal values, and vice versa. Therefore, as secularism becomes politically stronger in Israel, so will liberal values. A more secular Israel is a more liberal Israel. A more religious Israel is a more illiberal one. It is as simple as that. This is the choice.

Having badly defined the goal towards a "kinder, gentler" Jewish religion in the public sphere in Israel, American Jews have also chosen the least effective strategy possible. They have sought recognition for their brand of Judaism whether in matters of conversion, marriage, or prayer at the Kotel, from the very same authorities that have been given monopoly power over these matters by the State, principally, the Chief Rabbinate.

The Rabbinate will never, ever cede its power. No monopoly in the history of monopolies has ever given up or shared power voluntarily. Just ask AT&T. American Jews have been behaving like the frustrated customers of a corrupt monopoly. You do not ask a monopoly to treat you nicely. You break up a monopoly, with force.

Above all, if American Jews are to effect change in Israel to make room for their brand of pluralism, they need numbers. No political change is ever possible without numbers. And there are no numbers in Israel for the kind of Judaism that Americans have in America.

To get the big numbers, liberal American Jews have to decide who their actual potential allies are. If they seek Israeli Jews who will have a positive attitude towards religion, then they are likely to be non-liberal Orthodox Jews who reject their form of practice completely. If they seek Israeli Jews who will share their values of pluralism, equality, tolerance, feminism and liberalism, they are, by and large, likely to be the shrimp-eating-Shabbat-driving Jews, whose attitudes to religion range from revulsion to apathy.

If Conservative, Reform and generally liberal American Jews seek partners in Israel who share *both* their liberal values and positive attitude towards religion, they will limit themselves to a pool of citizens that is barely likely to get one seat in the Knesset.

Liberal American Jews have wasted hundreds of millions of dollars trying to shore up Reform and Conservative Judaism in Israel, to no avail. They celebrate the increase in numbers from next to nothing to a little more than nothing. But fundamentally Israel is not the soil for that kind of Judaism, which appeals almost exclusively to Olim from the West, who over time, revert to the dominant Zionist ethos.

As a result, American Jews have been financing micro-operations that will never be able to make a real impact on Israeli society. It is understandable that donors appreciate promoting the values they care for in the specific form they are accustomed to. But it has zero impact on Israeli society.

Worse, having long ago understood that they have no chance to convert religious Orthodox Israeli Jews to their kind of

79

pluralistic Judaism, American Jews have instead pivoted to trying to convert Israeli secular Jews to their brand of religion. The tragedy is that in doing so, they have unwittingly contributed to strengthening their religious Orthodox illiberal enemies.

Consider a parallel in the Second Amendment in America. Imagine an international organization seeking to convince NRA members to limit the exercise of the Second Amendment to pistols. Now imagine that once it becomes clear that America's gun-owning community would never warm up to limiting their love of guns to pistols, the organization instead redirects its energy towards convincing the Americans who loathe and fear guns to warm up to the idea of carrying pistols.

American Jews might recoil at the parallel between Jewish religion and guns. But in the Israeli context, that is the proper parallel. In Israel, the Jewish religion has been weaponized in the service of illiberalism and supremacism. Any support for religion of any kind only provides fuel for such values. This is what American Jews have been unwittingly supporting in the past several decades.

Illiberal Religion vs. Liberal Secularism

A prime example of this dangerous process has been the American Jewish support for the introduction of "additional" Jewish studies into secular schools. The Israeli school system is divided into several systems, determined by the level of religiosity of their communities. The religious schools promote strict, Orthodox practices and place a strong emphasis on Jewish religious studies. American Jews have no chance of penetrating this system to promote liberal values.

But the secular system is naturally open and liberal. So it has been the long-standing desire of the right wing religious coalition in Israel to eliminate this open and liberal character — since they consider it a threat to their illiberal and supremacist politics. Their most effective weapon, to that end, is to reduce as much as possible the study of general and universal humanities, in favor of an increased amount of Jewish studies.

In one of the greatest acts of self-defeating philanthropy, American Jews have underwritten numerous programs, both in schools and in informal education systems, intended to introduce "nice religious Judaism" into the curricula.

But there is no such thing in the Israeli context. Introducing religious studies to secular schools — even of the "nice" kind — contributes to a more religious Israel, and in Israel, Jewish religion cannot be dismantled from the Orthodox and illiberal manner in which it is practiced. This is the choice. If liberal American Jews want to be effective they need to understand the simple fact that in the Israeli Zionist context, the choice is between illiberal religion and liberal secularism. None other.

Instead of these self-defeating measures, *liberal American Jews should support all of the various battles actual Israelis, living in Israel, wage on behalf of greater secularization and less religion in public sphere.* This means resisting all efforts to introduce religion, of any kind, into Israel's public secular schools. This means fighting for the teaching of evolution. It means supporting the numerous grassroots efforts of Israeli parents to keep religion out of their children's schoolbooks, and to keep religious "volunteers" out of provision of extracurricular activities in school.

It also means supporting public transportation on Shabbat for those municipalities that seek it (imagine if in addition to having the names of donors on ambulances, they would be on buses providing services on Shabbat). It means supporting the promotion of full equality for LGBTQ citizens, especially on matters of family life. It means supporting the current legal battle against the prohibition on individuals bringing flour products into hospitals during Passover. It means especially standing firmly behind those who fight for the equality of women and men in the military and against any notion that "consideration for feelings" of religious soldiers should somehow come to mean discrimination against female soldiers.

American Jews need to also stop trying to get crumbs of recognition from the Chief Rabbinate. They should seek to sideline it completely. The goal should not be to get the state to allow Reform and Conservative Rabbis to perform marriages in Israel. The goal should not be an additional prayer area next to the Kotel. The goal should be breaking up the Rabbinate's monopoly altogether, on matters of conversion, marriage, Kashrut, and yes — the Kotel.

Secular Israelis are never going to politically mobilize, in great numbers, for the specific goal of the state of Israel funding Conservative and Reformed rabbis, or Conservative and Reformed Mikvahs. Secular Israelis want the state to not fund rabbis and Mikvahs at all.

In a secular Israel, liberal American Jews will have no problem finding a home for their brand of Jewish practice. In an Israel of civil unions, their rabbis, just like anyone else, will be able to perform ceremonies for those who want them. In a national, secular Kotel, American Jews will be able to pray how they want and see fit, because there will be no Rabbi to regulate them. In an Israel that doesn't fund rabbis and Mikvahs, any community that wants to fund their kind of religious services and practice would be able to do so.

This is the only kind of Israel that would be a home to all Jews, from all around the world. It is high time that American liberal Jews join forces with secular Israelis for a secular Zionist Israel. The future of the relationship between liberal American Jews and Israeli Jews depends on American Jews understanding the toxic role of religion in Israel, and redefining the goal — ruthlessly — towards a secular Israel.

ISRAEL DOESN'T NEED CONSERVATIVE OR REFORM JUDAISM

Response Op-Ed Co-Authored with Ram Vromen for Forward, August 2018

This summer, we wrote an article in these pages in which we argued that Reform and Conservative American Jews should stop importing their brand of Judaism to Israel on the grounds that we already have too much religion. What Israelis need is not softer versions of Judaism, but rather help strengthen our liberalism, which is under threat from the ultra-Orthodox Rabbinate and its enablers. There is no greater proof of the main thesis of our essay than the four essays written in response.

The responses focused on the importance of the liberal streams of Judaism. And yet, contrary to what the response essays argue, we are not seeking to erase or eliminate Reform and Conservative Jewish life in Israel. Our claim is merely that the political and public impact of these movements is minimal, and that the only way all forms of Jewish religious practice, including Reform and Conservative Judaism, can thrive in the Israeli public sphere is through a more secular Israel. Essential to the core of our argument is the fundamental difference between how Americans view religion and how Israelis do.

Religion in America has historically developed as a matter of personal choice subject to the same kinds of competitive dynamics you find at work in a capitalist society. Think about a Jew in America who's not pleased with their Rabbi's High Holidays sermon. They have numerous other synagogues to go to, or they can start a new one, or not go at all. Most importantly, once they step out of the synagogue or community center, they live in a country that at least makes an ongoing effort to separate religion and state.

Israelis have no such choice. *We have one Jewish state, which means that Judaism in Israel is not a matter of personal expression.* As much as some Israelis would like to, the option of seceding or creating other Jewish states that are more specifically catered to their worldview of how Judaism should be interpreted is not really an option. If we are to secure our freedom to practice Judaism however we want, we need to act politically and in the public sphere to do so. It is not a matter of individual choice. In the Jewish state, Judaism is a public and political matter.

This is hardly an argument for or against liberal Judaism, as some of the responses seemed to take it. We are sufficiently aware that Judaism, like all religious and ideological systems, is in the hands of its interpreters, and that its interpretation changes over times and geographies. As a millennia-old civilization, Judaism has produced enough texts, sayings, events and traditions to underpin a near infinite range of possibilities of personal expression, opinions and worldviews.

What we did argue was that *American Jews, thinking in American terms are pursuing the wrong strategy in seeking to make Israel more "pluralistic" in the very narrow sense of attaining official recognition for Reform and Conservative Judaism in Israeli political public sphere. It would be far more effective, we argued, to join hands with secular Israelis to secure an Israeli Zionist secular public sphere. In such an Israel, we wrote, liberal American Jews will have no problem finding a home for their brand of Jewish practice*:

"In an Israel of civil unions, their rabbis, just like anyone else, will be able to perform ceremonies for those who want them. In a national, secular Kotel, American Jews will be able to pray how they want and see fit, because there will be no Rabbi to regulate them. In an Israel that doesn't fund rabbis and Mikvehs, any community that wants to fund their kind of religious services and practice would be able to do so. This is the only kind of Israel that would be a home to all Jews, from all around the world."

Perhaps American Jews balk at the idea of going all in and backing secular Israeli struggles. Maybe they're afraid to take on the Rabbinate directly and to call for its downfall, or feel uneasy supporting public transportation on Shabbat in Israel or fighting against religious edicts in the Israeli military. Maybe they don't understand why it matters whether flour products may be brought into hospitals during Passover by individual patients.

And yet, even if our American Jewish brothers and sisters don't understand the importance of these secular measures, at the minimum, we ask that American Jews refrain from trying to import more religion — of whatever kind — into Israel.

There is no greater disservice that American liberal Jews can do for Israeli liberal Jews than import their brand of religion into Israel. This is a clear case of good intentions leading to bad outcomes, and this is what we seek to point out. For the truth of the matter is, in the Israeli context, more religion — of whatever kind — translates into greater illiberalism. Perhaps it is necessary to point out that Israeli Jews, even the most secular and militantly atheist among them, are not in need of more Judaism of any kind. And yet, it's hard not to notice the missionary tone of some of the essays responding to ours, which lamented that we are "cultivating ignorance and disconnect as an answer to religious fanaticism." Indeed, this is an argument that is no different than the one made by the most fanatic ultra-Orthodox about Zionist secularism. And the truth is, this is again to use an American paradigm to willfully misunderstand the Israeli context.

Ignorance and disconnect from Judaism is indeed possible and extant in the vast geographical and social planes of America. But it is a literal impossibility in Israel. It is practically impossible for any Jewish person (and most non-Jews too) to be ignorant of Judaism and disconnected from it in Israel.

Both of us wake up every morning, living our daily lives by the ancient Hebrew calendar. Shabbat is our day of rest. It is a day of national rest. Sunday is a day of work. Friday nights our respective families get together for dinner. Our holidays are the Jewish and Zionist holidays, and our families' arguments are about who will host which Jewish holiday, or whether it is better to flee abroad to avoid the arguments.

Our children go to public state kindergartens and schools, where Jewish holidays are a major part of their curriculum. With every approaching Jewish holiday (and there are many more than American Jews suspect), our children learn songs, write essays, discuss meanings, go on excursions, and make papier-mâché structures related to that holiday. In fact, we have to wonder what kindergarten teachers teach children in other parts of the world without Jewish holidays.

Throughout their school years, our children learn the Hebrew Bible, medieval Hebrew poetry, ancient and modern history of the Jewish people (they always tried to kill us, even when they didn't...), modern Zionist thought and history and Hebrew literature. When our children attend their after-school activities, their soccer team is called Maccabi, and their youth movement discussions are about the essence and dilemmas of living in the Jewish state. Even if Israelis wanted to, and they indeed don't, they could not send "their kids to schools devoid of Jewish culture and spirit", as one response essay argues.

Indeed, while our children go to their public schools and kindergartens and after school activities, we browse the news, read our Twitter and Facebook feeds and engage in daily heated debates about the current iteration of what it means to be the Jewish state.

We debate the Nation State Bill, the boycott, divestment and sanctions movement against Israel, the closure of public construction on Shabbat. We ask whether the ultra-Orthodox should serve in the army, whether Israeli soldiers be allowed to use their cell phones on Shabbat, whether the occupation is justified if it's in defense of Jewish life, or whether it's an occupation at all, or the end of the Jewish state. We debate whether the new natural history museum in Israel should have exhibits about evolution.

And when we take a break from the news to entertain ourselves, we watch Fauda, a TV show about Israeli soldiers undercover as Arabs, or Autonomia, a series about a future where Israel splits into a Haredi autonomy and a Zionist state, or Shababnikim, a show about young Haredi Jews. Or we go out to see the film "Unorthodox", about the rise of the Mizrahi Haredi movement Shas.

And, miracles of miracles, we do all that in Hebrew – reading, writing and speaking the modern iteration of the ancient language of our people. All this is even without mentioning that in our professional lives we both spend all our time on Zionist and Jewish issues. In truth, *even if we wanted to have "more Judaism" in our lives, as all of the response writers seem to imply we are lacking, we would hardly know when and where to insert it.*

This is the essential difference between Jewish life in America and in Israel. In America, Jewish life has to be actively pursued, if it is to exist at all. If it is not actively pursued, the baseline is indeed one of "ignorance and disconnect."

For Jews in Israel, Judaism is woven into the very fabric of our lives, in every second and every act. The fact that it may not resemble what Americans call Judaism doesn't make it any less so; it just makes it different. As a colleague in Israel who made Aliyah from Canada likes to say, the day that he moved to Israel, he stopped keeping kosher. In the Israeli context, it became superfluous.

Liberal American Jews need exhibit no concern whatsoever for Judaism in Israel. What they need to do is exhibit substantial concern for liberalism in Israel Israelis don't need more Judaism, cultural, religious, historical, lingual, ritual or otherwise. What many Israelis need and want is more liberalism, and in the Israeli context more liberalism can only come with greater secularism.

And in the Israeli Zionist context greater liberalism will be secured only through greater secularism. Greater secularism doesn't mean less Judaism, but rather, pushing back on the expansionist policies of illiberal Jewish Orthodoxy. It is a matter of power – not a matter of ritual or culture.

Once American Jews accept that the Israeli Zionist operating system is fundamentally different than the American one, and that they should abandon their proselytizing project of injecting more religion, in any form, into the Israeli public space, they will finally be able to tap into the most important resource of power that exists in Israel to oppose Orthodox illiberalism: Zionist secularism.

Despite the efforts of the response writers to depict a rise in Reform and Conservative Judaism in Israel, absent an Aliyah of millions of American Jews, those are and will remain marginal phenomena. It's true that there's a growing number of Israelis who support these movements. But it is mostly because secular Israelis view Reform and Conservative Judaism as doing battle against a shared enemy: illiberal Orthodoxy and the Chief Rabbinate.

Indeed, this affection for the liberal streams of Judaism should not be mistaken for adherence. For this sympathy and affection end when the religious aspects of these movements come into play. Take, for example, a school in Tel Aviv which was always on the secular forefront, and threw out the Orthodox organization that used to teach Judaism in the school back in 2016, a full year before all the other schools in Tel Aviv did so. The school replaced the Orthodox teachers with an organization belonging to the Reform movement. But rather than solving the problem, this resulted in complaints by parents that the new solution was all too similar to the old one. It, too, highlighted religious, and even missionary, content. After another year, the Reform organization was shown the door.

Only Zionist secularism can muster the numbers, intensity, and local historical resonance needed for a successful political struggle for liberal values. In independent polls, secular Israelis still represent over 40% of Israeli society. The fact that this plurality has been silent is the outcome of the fact that for many decades, secular Zionism was indeed the politically hegemonic force in Israel. With the growing realization that this is no longer the case, and that secular Zionists need to actively fight again for their way of life and values, secular Zionists are speaking up and acting.

Finally, the writers of the response essays suggest that we are ignoring the vast middle of Mizrahi Jews and Israeli Jews of Russian background, as if those groups could somehow be a resource of support for the Conservative and Reform brand of Judaism. One should not make the mistake of taking the tolerance of Mizrahi Jews towards mild levels of Jewish ritual practice as any form of sympathy for Reform and Conservative Judaism. Quite the opposite: Traditional Mizrahi Jews, as a rule, are sometimes more vigorous than the strictly religious in sanctifying Orthodox Judaism and opposing pluralist movements, which they see as "left wing." And Israeli Jews of Russian background are first and foremost Israeli. They do not identify with forms of Judaism that are not identifiably Israeli and will therefore operate within the Israeli Jewish Orthodox/ secular dichotomy. They tend to be either firm atheists or worshippers of Orthodox Judaism, due to political reasons. Neither group is interested in the American import of liberal Judaism, which is as distant from them as Christianity.

In America, American Jews can be whatever kind of Jews they want. But when American Jews seek to have an impact in Israel, in a direction of greater liberal values, and especially greater acceptance and recognition of their own form of Jewish life and practice, their best political allies are secular Israelis.

HERE IS WHY SO MANY ARE OUTRAGED BY ISRAEL'S NATION-STATE LAW

Essay co-authored with Shany Mor for Mosaic Magazine, October 2018

Why all the outrage over Israel's nation-state law?," ask, innocently, Moshe Koppel and Eugene Kontorovich in *Mosaic*. The answer is: context. Just as Koppel and Kontorovich don't trust Israel's "activist and politically-biased [Supreme] Court" to interpret properly any law that would enshrine the broad concept of "equality"—thereby admitting that context matters immensely to them, too—we don't trust this Israeli government and this law's political promoters to interpret Zionism properly.

Only one article in the nation-state law truly matters and entails clear political consequences. It is article 1(c): "The exercise of the right to national self-determination in the state of Israel is *unique*[our emphasis] to the Jewish people." All other articles flow from this one.

In one context, this statement embodies the essence of Zionism and the state of Israel. As a proposal for enshrining the Jewishness of the state *in part of* the historic Land of Israel, with an overwhelming Jewish majority and an unimpeachably democratic regime, the text of the Basic Law: Nation-State is generally acceptable and reflects the broad consensus of Israel's Jewish Zionist majority. Indeed, nothing about Jewish self-determination is especially unique or uniquely bad. In another context, however—the one envisioned by the law's recent promoters—the law becomes a proposal for entrenching, against any possible democratic challenge, Jewish supremacy in a regime covering the entire Land of Israel with a bare 50-percent Jewish majority, if that. In this context, the law is entirely unacceptable.

The text may be the same text, but the context is radically different, and so would be its application. In effect, the declarative import of the law will have moved from affirming one people's liberation to endeavoring to preserve another's subjugation. Hence the outrage.

Between the Jordan River and the Mediterranean Sea live millions of people who belong, broadly, to two collectives. Whatever either one thinks about the other, and however "invented" either one deems the other's nature, they rather violently agree that one is not the other. We ourselves believe, and it is the general global spirit of the last century, that these millions of people have the universal right to be sovereign masters of their fate. They can do so in one polity or more.

We, proud members of the Jewish collective, who believe that the purpose of Zionism was not to create a concentrated Jewish minority in a majority-Arab Muslim state, prefer that the Jewish people be sovereign in a state of their own, and that the Arab Palestinians exercise sovereignty in a state of their own as well. As the numbers stand, this means partition: dividing the land between the two collectives so that each enjoys a solid and overwhelming majority in a state of its own. This is the only path that enables *all* the millions of people living between the River and the Sea to exercise sovereignty.

In this context, the context of partition, article 1(c) is perfectly fine. It is even necessary. It makes it clear that the very purpose of the painful act of partition is indeed to secure, for generations to come, the one state in the world where "the right to self-determination is unique to the Jewish people" while also adhering to the founding vision of a state based, in the words of its Declaration of Independence, "on freedom, justice, and peace as envisaged by the prophets of Israel."

But if in the state of Israel the Jewish collective is uniquely entitled to exercise its right to self-determination, as is proper, it follows that the only way the Arab Palestinians, the members of the other collective, can exercise their own universal right to be

WE SHOULD ALL BE ZIONISTS

sovereign in some polity is to have self-determination in a state of their own.

This is why one of us, Einat Wilf, while a member of the Knesset, and in the wake of Prime Minister Benjamin Netanyahu's 2009 speech at Bar Ilan University in support of the two-state solution, signed and defended the then-proposed bill in its early round; indeed, as much as Netanyahu now denies it, his government was at that time actively negotiating partition. And this is also why Wilf continues to defend the same text in the now-passed law—on the condition, however, that Israel simultaneously and publicly delineate its final eastern border along a mildly altered 1967 line—and why Shany Mor has likewise defended the text against its more hysterical critics. But this is emphatically not the vision of the law's promoters. They—most notably, Justice Minister Ayelet Shaked, Tourism Minister Yariv Levin, and Environment Minister Zeev Elkin—are vocal opponents of Arab-Palestinian self-determination. They are on record, frequently and repeatedly, rejecting any division of sovereignty in the land between the River and the Sea. Worse, they are known promoters of plans to annex the entire West Bank while permanently denying any path by which the Arab Palestinians living there could ever gain sovereignty and become masters of their fate. (Yes, the rejectionists' plans do speak of annexing "only" 60 percent of the West Bank, known in the Oslo Agreements as Area C. But that is a fraud. There is no such thing as a single "Area C." Instead, there are numerous small areas bearing the designation "C"; in practice, annexing them would mean annexing the entire West Bank while excluding the Arab Palestinians living in dozens of enclaves there from participation in the rights of the annexing power. Calling this "autonomy on steroids," as some have done, is no help; unlike the situation in autonomous regions elsewhere, the inhabitants would still be denied participation in the sovereign polity that determines their fate.)

In this context,it becomes clear why annexationists like Shaked, Levin, and Elkin cannot abide a guarantee of "equality" in any basic law: given the numbers, equal citizenship for all Arab Palestinians living between the River and the Sea would spell the end of sovereignty for the Jewish people. For our part, we, too, like most Israeli Jews, fear equality under conditions of annexation—again, however, not because we distrust Israel's "activist and politically-biased [Supreme] Court" but because it would spell the literal end of Zionism.

The reason that Israeli Jewish annexationists must oppose equality is that their plan can be carried out only through the denial of Arab Palestinian rights, either to self-determination in a state of their own or as equal citizens in the state of Israel. From this perspective, the constitutional victory heralded by the law's promoters has little to do with the Supreme Court itself; after all, none other than Ayelet Shaked recently told the *Atlantic* that Israel's "conservative camp can no longer whine about being underrepresented" in the courts. Instead, it has almost everything to do with the West Bank settler movement, which has gradually redefined Zionism from a movement for the self-determination of the Jewish people in its historic homeland to an affirmation of a theocratically based regime lording it over a non-Jewish majority. There is a name for this, and the name is supremacism: specifically, Jewish supremacism.

Koppel and Kontorovich might seek to allay our fears and mitigate our resistance by saying, as they have done in conversation, that the issue of annexation is a separate matter and we should fight for partition regardless of the nation-state law. *But we have no intention of legitimizing the explosive legal foundation that the law provides for promoting the annexationist position*. The supremacists' Zionism is not ours, and the Israel they are busy preparing is so distant from the ideals of Israel's founders that we vow to fight it every step of the way. Hence the outrage.

WE ARE STILL A MINORITY IN THE REGION

Op-Ed for Newsweek, May 2021

Israel and Hamas have agreed to a cease-fire. As of Friday morning, Israelis can now emerge from safe rooms and communal shelters across the country. But while this round of fighting was short by some standards, lasting just 11 days, its impact could last much longer. For the barrage of attacks from Gaza was accompanied by intense Arab violence *within* Israel, for the first time in decades.

Throughout this latest round of fighting, Arab Israelis **pillaged and vandalized** Jewish property in what are known as "mixed" Arab and Jewish towns such as Akko, Haifa, Lod, and Ramle. In some cases, they engaged in brutal and deadly lynching. While there were also attacks by Jewish Israeli mobs, the overwhelming number of attacks were carried out by Arab youths.

Far more than the attacks from Gaza, *these attacks within Israel's borders touched the deepest historical fears of Israel's Jews and enforced our sense of being under siege. And they reminded us of something that few outside of Israel seem to understand: Despite representing the majority of the citizens living within the sovereign territory of Israel Jews, many Jewish Israelis view themselves as a minority amidst an Arab majority.*

These mental frames are the result of both history and geography. Historically, Jews have been shaped as a people by the experience of being a minority—a persecuted one—while Arabs have been shaped by the experience of being a dominant majority across the Middle East.

It's hard to overestimate the depth of the impact this has had. Much of what is considered typical of Jewish life, from holiday rituals to culture to humor, has been shaped by the persistent historical experience of being a minority in danger. Jews are deeply cognizant of their numerical vulnerability, which is no theoretical matter. Precisely because Jews are so few, they have historically existed at the mercy of the majority peoples among whom they've resided. When that numerical majority was kind to the Jews, Jews prospered, and when the numerical majority no longer has an interest in having Jews in its midst, expulsions, pogroms and genocide followed.

The Nazi Final Solution to the Jewish Question put this numerical vulnerability of the Jewish people in its most stark—and literal—form: When Nazi leaders gathered in the serene Villa Wannsee to develop the Final Solution, they methodically listed the number of Jews living in each of the territories controlled by the Nazis across Europe and in the recently invaded Soviet Union. Even territories that were still unconquered by Nazis like England were listed. 48,000 Jews in Bulgaria were listed with the 1,300 Jews of Norway and the 2,994,684 Jews of The Ukraine. And in a neat column, the numbers of all the Jews were added up to yield 11,000,000. It was a number that clearly appeared doable to the Nazis. They were able to conceive of a Final Solution to the Jewish Question in the form of industrial mass extermination precisely because to them, the total number of Jews was such that the operation could be carried out. And indeed, within three short years, the Nazis had efficiently completed more than half their goal.

This sense of historical vulnerability is enhanced by geography. While Jews are the numerical majority within the State of Israel, zooming out into the region reveals they are a tiny minority in a predominantly Arab and Islamic region, in which generally unarmed minorities are doomed to expulsion or massacres.

Again, this has not been a theoretical concept for Jews. Despite taking no part in war, Jews were completely expelled from across the Arab and Islamic Middle East and North Africa when the Arab failure to strangle a nascent Israel in 1948 created the risk that Jews might become uppity and no longer "know their place" as the Dhimmi subservient peoples as they were for centuries under Islam. Within a decade, Jewish communities, which predated the conquests of Islam, were gone.

And this experience is something Arabs just do not have, at least not in the Middle East. Ever since the Arab conquests turned the region and North Africa into Muslim and Arab, Arabs and Muslims have been the dominant and even exclusive majority across the region. And while there have been conflicts between the Sunni and Shiite sects, these are a far cry from a tiny minority living amongst another alien religion.

This makes Israel unique, in that it's a country where Arabs live as a minority. It thus represents the "natural" order of things upended, and so it does not matter that Arabs are full citizens of Israel in a country that meets the **European Union** standards for the equal treatment of national minorities (language, education, holidays); the natural order must be restored. But Israel is unique in another way: It remains one of the few countries in the world that is home to a national minority that belongs to a regional majority at war with the country in which they live.

Just consider how Western countries treated their citizens of Japanese and German descent during WWII, or how they treated Communists during the Cold War, to get a sense of what it means for Israel's Jews to live with a substantial Arab minority over decades of never-ending war and conflict with the Arab world.

Understanding this minority-majority inversion is critical to grasping the paradox that stumps many observers of Israel, even the sympathetic ones, of what appears like a massive gap between Israel's military and economic power and the overwhelming sense of vulnerability that pervades Israeli Jewish thinking. Zooming out resolves this tension: It is our numerical vulnerability in the region that we feel so deeply, that demands we build our military and economic might to prevent the overwhelming majority in the region from successfully acting on its numerical dominance, as it has on multiple occasions.

In recent months, The Trump-brokered Abraham Accords, the quiet on all fronts and the prospect of Arab-Jewish political cooperation created a palpable sense that Israel's Jews might finally be emerging from decades of siege and could finally live in the region while maintaining sovereignty, rather than as a minority at the mercy of others. But the events of the past few weeks have pierced that sense that Israeli Jews could leave behind their existence as a besieged minority in a hostile region. Israeli Jews were forced to confront the reality that it is still possible to unite large parts of the Arab and Islamic world (and their allies) against the fundamental grievance of Jewish power and self-determination, of which all other stated grievances are but symptoms.

Perhaps with time and with exhaustion, Arab acceptance of Jewish self-determination in the region will finally enable Jews in Israel to exhibit the confidence and openness of a comfortable majority in their own state and free Arabs to become a truly integrated minority in a Jewish state. Until that time, we may ponder the particular majority-minority aspects of Jewish-Arab relations in Israel and the region and marvel that the situation is not far far worse.

ISRAELI ARAB MK MANSOUR ABBAS IS WHAT ZIONISM INTENDED

Essay for The State of Tel Aviv with research by Samuel Hyde, June 2022

In June 2021 for the first time ever, an Arab political party, Ra'am, joined a governing coalition in Israel. Equally extraordinary is the fact that Ra'am, led by Mansour Abbas, is a conservative, Islamic party aligned with the Muslim Brotherhood. Supporters of the coalition, mainly from the Center and Left, praised what they saw as the fuller realization of a liberal Jewish state. Yesh Atid leader and newly minted Foreign Minister Yair Lapid spoke of a "change to the history books." "The Arab public," affirmed Labor party leader Merav Michaeli, "is part of Israeli society." And Naftali Bennett, the new prime minister and head of the right-wing Yamina party, called Abbas a "unifier."

In stark contrast, the right-wing opposition issued warnings of impending doom for the Jewish state. They assailed Abbas as a sly politician working to destroy the Jewish state from within. Benjamin Netanyahu (who had also courted Abbas when trying to cobble together a government) declared that the new coalition "will be celebrated in Tehran, Ramallah, and in Gaza, just as they celebrate every terror attack. But," he warned, "this will be a national historic terror attack on the State of Israel from within."

According to Netanyahu and his supporters, Ra'am and Abbas had not "accepted" the Jewish state, but merely changed tactics. Having failed to defeat Israel through decades of wars, terrorism, violence and global propaganda campaigns, Netanyahu asserted, Ra'am was spearheading an effort on behalf of Arabs and Muslims to subvert the Jewish state.

So – which is it? Real change as heralded by the Left? Or a sinister masquerade as characterized by the Right? This question, clearly, is acutely important.

Abbas represents a radical break with decades of Israeli-Arab refusal to join an Israeli government coalition. Yet, his party is also loyal to the Muslim Brotherhood, which is the parent movement of Hamas and other sworn enemies of Israel.

Either way, the stakes could hardly be higher. The dilemma puts in sharp relief the two dichotomous possibilities: that Abbas's politics represent the realization of the vision of pre-state Zionist thinkers or that the survival of the Jewish state is gravely threatened.

I. MANSOUR ABBAS: "ISRAEL IS A JEWISH STATE"

Unlike his predecessors, Mansour Abbas skillfully and genuinely dealt with challenges that made it otherwise impossible for Arab politicians to participate in governing coalitions. He openly acknowledged and accepted Israel as a Jewish state.

Faced with a wave of terror attacks this past spring, some of which were carried out by Arab citizens of Israel, Abbas' repeated condemnations of these attacks contrasted starkly with signs carried by protesters at a Likud rally reading: "Abbas is a terrorist and supports terrorism against the Jewish state."

In the immediate aftermath of a terror attack on civilians in Hadera, Abbas said it was "a despicable display of ISIS terrorism that does not represent Arab society within Israel." Israeli-Arabs, he said, "seek a dignified life within the rule of law and a value system that sanctifies human life. Arab and Jewish co-existence, and the values of peace and tolerance."

As tensions and violence between Israeli soldiers and Palestinians escalated on the highly sensitive location of the Temple Mount and Al-Aqsa Mosque, Abbas very soberly addressed the situation, saying that while "the scenes at Al-Aqsa were very difficult, it doesn't matter how it started or how it ended." He added that he "put out a call for calm and to give [the mosque] its respect, to allow people to pray in peace." Again, he wasted no time in making his statement.

Abbas was bold enough to raise the *ante* yet again when he stated clearly in December 2021 that: "Israel was born as a Jewish state. It was born that way and that's how it will remain... the question is how we integrate Arab society into it." Such unqualified acceptance of Israel by an Arab political leader is unprecedented.

Nor was this statement a "one-off." Again and again, Abbas made it clear that his goal was to deliver tangible results for his voters. "I want to maintain the hope for Arab society," he said, "[that] we'll achieve our goals of full social equality and a society that is prosperous and a partner in decision making." Indeed, during the one year of this government's existence, substantial funds were allocated to many issues of particular concern to Israel's Arab citizens, including infrastructure, education, and a significant reduction in violent crime.

II. ZE'EV JABOTINSKY PREDICTED MANSOUR ABBAS AND THE IRON WALL

The Zionist leader who most directly considered the issue as to whether Jews and Arabs could be true partners in a liberal democracy was Ze'ev Jabotinsky in his 1923 essay, "The Iron Wall."

Jabotinsky was one of the foremost thinkers and leaders of early Zionism. He is perhaps best known for having founded the right-wing Revisionist movement which considered the exercise of Jewish power – militarily and politically – to be imperative if a nation was to be built. Jabotinsky was revered both by his political opponents, such as Israel's first prime minister, David Ben-Gurion, and by fiercely loyal followers, including his protégé and future prime minister, Menachem Begin.

Contrary to the caricature of early Zionist thought by its detractors, their vision for a Jewish state was never one of Jewish exclusivity. Whether it was Theodor Herzl, Jabotinsky, or the leaders of Labor Zionism, they all understood that ever since the Arab and Islamic conquests of the land in the seventh century, a large cohort of the local population was Muslim or Christian by religion and Arab by language and culture. All visions of the Jewish state included the Arabs of the land as equal citizens and governors of the Jewish state.

To the extent they differed, it was on how this vision would be realized. Herzl assumed, given that the Zionists' intentions were to work and develop the land rather than exploit it, that the Arabs who lived in the sparsely populated and underdeveloped region would enthusiastically welcome the Jews.

Jabotinsky, however, recognized that regardless of the good intentions of the Zionists, the local population would resist a growing Jewish presence. Countering Arab resistance necessitated Jewish power. He questioned whether "peaceful aims could be achieved by peaceful means." Only if the Zionists had the capability to repel such resistance – erecting an "Iron Wall" – would the Arabs of the land finally come to accept them.

While Herzl's naïve assessment of "no resistance" was probably essential to mobilize the youthful optimism of the early Zionists, Jabotinsky articulated the practical imperatives for the movement to succeed. The establishment of a Jewish state, he maintained, necessitated the exercise of Jewish power.

Israel's commitment to military, economic and diplomatic power derived from the Iron Wall theory. Herzl envisioned the path to a Jewish state. Jabotinsky envisioned the path to Arab acceptance of that state.

But even the more hard-headed *Jabotinsky did not believe that the Zionists were destined to always live by the sword. Once the Arabs truly accepted the existence of the Jewish state, Jews and Arabs would govern together. On the other side of the Iron Wall, he believed in a highly liberal vision for the emergent state where "in every Cabinet where the prime minister is a Jew, the vice-premiership shall be offered to an Arab, and vice-versa."*

But Jabotinsky underestimated the magnitude, ferocity, and persistence of the Arabs' violent rejection of Zionism. When he first called for the mounting of an Iron Wall, there were about 10 million Jews in Europe and Asia and several hundred thousand Arabs in the land itself. Through immigration, he believed, the

Jews would ultimately constitute the overwhelming majority in the fledgling state. (For this reason, Jabotinsky's liberal vision of an alternating Jewish and Arab Prime Minister was not a vision of bi-nationalism based on numerical parity. It was still a vision of a Jewish state, just a liberal one.)

Jabotinsky could not have foreseen that the devastating convergence of the rise of Nazism, World War II and Arab violence in Mandatory Palestine would cause the British to choke off Jewish migration, at the most desperate time. This meant that millions of Jews, who could have otherwise immigrated to the embryonic Jewish state, were left to perish in Europe. The possibility of a Jewish majority in the entire territory allocated to the future Jewish state by the League of Nations Mandate, as envisioned by Jabotinsky and other Zionists, would be deferred, perhaps indefinitely. As a result, the Iron Wall would have to persist much longer than he had hoped.

Nearly a century after Jabotinsky wrote "The Iron Wall," does Mansour Abbas herald its success? Has Israel's continuous display of power finally caused its Arab population to accept its core identity as a Jewish state?

There is a parallel development in Israel's relations with neighboring Arab states. The 2020 *Abraham Accords* certainly suggest that Jabotinsky's model worked. This was the view set out by the Israeli Ambassador to the United States, Mike Herzog, speaking at a JINSA event (Jewish Institute for National Security of America) in January 2021, stating:

It was only due to the uncompromising willpower behind the Iron Wall and Israel's refusal to bend the knee to its neighboring enemies that it later became an appealing partner for others in the Arab world against the mutual threat of Iran.

But does the same rationale also guide Israel's Arab citizens and their political representatives?

III. THE CURIOUS POLITICAL PARALLELS OF ISRAELI-ARABS AND THE ULTRA-ORTHODOX

Upon Israel's founding, two groups which did not share its Zionist vision became part of the state of Israel: the Haredi Ultra-Orthodox Jews and the Arabs living in Mandatory Palestine. Arab and Haredi political parties, nevertheless, were quick to grasp the importance of ensuring that they had political representation in Israel's Parliament, the Knesset, and became active participants in the democratic life of the Zionist Jewish state.

But while both Haredim and Arabs opposed Zionism, the relationship between Israel's Jewish majority and its Arab minority was even more fraught. Following their defeat in the 1948 war against the establishment of Israel, Arabs were suddenly citizens of the new state they had just fought violently to destroy. Moreover, while Jews established themselves as a majority within Israel's sovereign territory, they remained a miniscule ethnic, national, religious and linguistic minority in a region overwhelmingly dominated by Arab culture and Islam. Israeli-Arabs shared a sense of identity, belonging and cultural affiliation with the dominant Arab and Muslim nations of the region – which collectively remained sworn enemies of the Jewish state.

And so, while Israel's Arab citizens had the right to vote and be elected to the Knesset from the outset, the continued ideological opposition of the Israeli-Arab population to the existence and legitimacy of a Jewish state and their identification with Israel's mortal enemies, meant that for more than seven decades Arab political parties were not part of any governing coalition.

Haredi parties, like Israeli-Arabs, were ideologically opposed to Zionism, but because their opposition was never violent they were able to chart a different course to political participation, joining governing coalitions, serving as deputy ministers with ministerial authority (but not serving officially as ministers in the government until a recent legal ruling compelled one of them to do so). They were thus able to leverage their political representation in the Knesset to secure policies and legislation beneficial to their voters, without officially compromising their ideological opposition to Zionism.

It would take Israel's Arab citizens more than seven decades to produce a political party that would follow the Haredi path of balancing politics and ideology. That party is Ra'am.

IV. A NEW TYPE OF ISRAELI ARAB LEADER

In March 2021, Mansour Abbas broke with more than 70 years of Israeli-Arab political parties' rejection of open political cooperation with Zionism. Instead, he ran on a platform echoing the traditional Haredi formula of seeking participation in Israel's ruling coalition, if not its government. Abbas declared that he is "a man of the Islamic Movement, a proud Arab and Muslim, a citizen of the State of Israel who heads the leading, biggest political movement in Arab society. What we have in common is greater than what divides us."

Abbas' unprecedented political gamble paid off. He was able to clear the parliamentary threshold to command four seats in Israel's 120-member Knesset. While that may not sound like much, Abbas had already announced before the final election results were in that he was willing to join any governing coalition – Left or Right. His party, he said, "was not obligated to any bloc or any candidate. We are not in anyone's pocket, not on the Right and not on the Left."

Abbas repeatedly made it clear that his goal – like that of the Haredi parties – was to deliver tangible achievements to his constituency. "I want to maintain the hope for Arab society," he said, "[that] we'll achieve our goals of full social equality and a society that is prosperous and a partner in decision making."

Abbas cemented his kingmaker position when he was seriously courted by Benjamin Netanyahu in the latter's fourth, failed effort in two years to establish a governing coalition. This may have seemed counterintuitive – it was traditionally the position of the Left to support inclusion for Arab representatives. But Netanyahu's signal that Likud also endorsed this approach was a game changer, opening the way to an unprecedented Right-Center-Left coalition that included Ra'am – and not Netanyahu.

Ironically, Abbas indicated that his party and constituents felt more comfortable with the conservative and religious coalition of Netanyahu than with the secular, LGBTQ+ supporters of the Left. "What have I to do with the Left?" he asked, pointedly. "In foreign policy we support the two-state solution, but in religious matters, I'm right-wing."

Abbas further facilitated the process of Ra'am's entry into the coalition by abandoning the traditional militant anti-Zionist stance of Israel's Arab parties. Immediately after being elected to parliament, he quoted verses from the Quran in Hebrew, calling for the creation of "an opportunity for a shared life, in the holy and blessed land for the followers of the three religions and both peoples. Now is the time for change." He adopted the Haredi message of caring for his constituents, leaving aside the conflict with the Palestinians.

All of which begs the question: Does Mansour Abbas' personal conduct and the partial acceptance of Ra'am's message among Israel's Arab citizens confirm the success of Jabotinsky's Iron Wall?

V. IS THE IRON WALL NEEDED FOREVER?

Israel is closer today than it has ever been in its history to realizing the goal of full acceptance in a predominantly Arab and Islamic region. The Abraham Accords present a compelling alternative Arab-Muslim narrative, one that embraces the Jewish state as an integral part of the region rather than a foreign implant.

Similarly, Mansour Abbas has given political voice to the Arab citizens of Israel who seek true integration into the Jewish state. Those are the Arab citizens who are volunteering in increasing numbers to serve in Israel's Defense Forces. Those are the Arab citizens who defend Israel in diplomatic forums and on social media against its detractors.

These developments reflect very real achievements of Jabotinsky's Iron Wall. Many Arab Israelis do not seek the country's destruction. They support and participate in its success.

But these achievements remain fragile. Abbas' political rival among Israel's Arab political leaders, Ayman Odeh, leader of the Joint List (an alignment of Arab parties), recently told young Israeli-Arabs not to join the "occupation forces." Odeh described Abbas' conduct as being "insulting and humiliating" and called on those who already serve in the security forces to "throw the weapons in their (the Israelis') face and tell them that our place is not with you."

Odeh represents a substantial number of Israel's Arab citizens, if not its majority. This complex situation is best summed up by Abbas himself who, criticizing his colleagues, called on them "to not look at the half-empty cup but at what we have achieved so far."

The Iron Wall, as applied through a century of the Zionist movement, has led to great achievements, but the process continues. The IDF will be needed for the foreseeable future, and the Jewish state must continue to be vigilant regarding those who would celebrate its demise, from without and within. Israel must insist that it be embraced as the Jewish state, rather than allow for the negation of this core principle of its nationhood. While positive signs of acceptance need to be celebrated, it would be unwise to ignore or explain away indications to the contrary.

Ultimately, Jabotinsky best combined the realism of necessary strength with a hopeful vision of peace based on Arab acceptance of the Jewish state. Those two goals – strength and peace – remain the twin pillars grounding the reality and vision of the Jewish state.

III. What do Palestinians Really Want?

THE FATAL FLAW THAT DOOMED THE OSLO ACCORDS

Op-Ed for The Atlantic, September 2018

It hardly seems possible that it's been 25 years since the signing of the Oslo Accords, that hopeful moment when peace between Palestinians and Israelis seemed at hand. In retrospect, the Accords seem less a triumph than an abject failure. Most observers, trying to understand what went wrong, fight over who to blame. The more constructive question is not who, but rather what, to blame. *What doomed the Oslo Accords is also what made them possible in the first place: constructive ambiguity.*

Given decades of war and bloodshed, the theory went, the two sides could not be expected to immediately settle their core disputes; an interim period of trust-building was required. It was better to remain ambiguous about the core issues which needed to be resolved, the negotiators assumed, rather than force the sides to adopt positions and make concessions which they might not be ready to make.

This constructive ambiguity, imbued in each element of the Accords, proved to be utterly destructive. Instead of building trust and allowing the parties to adjust to the reality of the inevitable compromises which were necessary for peace, it merely allowed each side to persist in its own self-serving interpretation of what the Accords implied and to continue the very behavior which destroyed trust on the other side. And so, when the time came, a few short years later, to settle the core issues, the ensuing failure was all but inevitable. Throughout the interim years of the Oslo Accords, Israeli settlement activity was allowed to continue unhampered, with the number of settlers increasing from 110,000 on the eve of the Accords in 1993 to 185,000 in 2000, during the negotiations over a final status, to 430,000 today. That increase seriously undermined the notion that Israel was sincere about making way for a Palestinian state in the West Bank and Gaza.

Palestinian leaders, meanwhile, continued pursuing what they referred to as the "Right of Return," their demand that ever-growing numbers of Palestinians be allowed to settle within the territory of pre-1967 Israel, which would render Jews a minority in an Arab state. There were nearly 3 million Palestinians registered with UNRWA as refugees in 1993, a number that increased to 3.8 million in 2000, and which stands at 5.3 million today. Palestinian leaders never dared face their people to tell them that as part of a final peace agreement, just as Jews would be expected to vacate their settlements east of the pre-1967 lines, Arab Palestinians be expected to renounce their claim to settle west of those lines. Like settlement building, this undermined the notion that Arab Palestinians had finally made their peace with the presence of a sovereign Jewish people in any part of the land. These two grand obstacles to peace—Israeli settlements and the Right of Return—each representing a form of territorial maximalism and the ideological negation of the other people's right to self-determination in the land, grew ever larger under the umbrella of constructive ambiguity.

Jerusalem, too, fell prey to destructive ambiguity. Israeli leaders continued to peddle the lie of a "united Jerusalem," failing to prepare Israelis for the necessary partition of Jerusalem into an Israeli capital and a Palestinian one, and Palestinian leaders extended their decades-long rejection of the idea that Jews have any historical, cultural, national, or religious connection to Jerusalem. Twenty-five years after that hopeful Oslo moment, there is no need to rethink the end goal—but we need a new path to get there. The two-state solution remains the only option that recognizes the national rights of both peoples and provides a measure of justice to each. Whatever each side thinks about the invented nature of the other, both sides can agree that they each are equally deserving of living in a state where they can be masters of their own fate.

To get there, the parties need to approach the negotiations not as a marriage, but as a divorce. Serious peacemakers need to let go of vague and nebulous concepts such as "trust" and "confidence building," and behave more like harsh divorce attorneys who spell out every detail. In place of destructive ambiguity, we need constructive specificity. President Trump, for example, would have done Israelis, Palestinians, and the cause of peace a greater favor if, rather than using the ambiguous term "Jerusalem," he had recognized only *west* Jerusalem as the capital of Israel, while making it clear that he is open to recognizing Arab *east* Jerusalem as the capital of Palestine. President Obama would actually have served the cause of peace if he had coupled his promotion of the UN Security Council Resolution 2334, which made it clear that Jews should not settle *east* of the pre-1967 line, with an equally stringent resolution that made it clear that Palestinians could not settle *west* of the pre-1967 line through the demand of return, condemning both forms of maximalism as illegitimate and harmful to a negotiated and just peace.

Repeated rounds of negotiations for a final-status agreement, especially in 2000, with the Clinton parameters, and in 2008, under Israeli Prime Minister Ehud Olmert, have served to specify parameters of a peace agreement between Israel and the Palestinians. It would require both parties to make considerable compromises, but offer both of them a viable sovereign state and the right of self-determination: a Palestinian state in the West Bank and Gaza, Jewish Jerusalem as the capital of Israel, Arab Jerusalem as the capital of Palestine, and a special arrangement in the Holy Basin to secure freedom of worship for all; annexation of major Jewish settlement blocs adjacent to the Green Line in exchange for swaps of equivalent land; removal of all other settlements from the West Bank; and enabling Palestinians living in Jordan, Syria, and Lebanon, to settle into a new State of Palestine—not into Israel. Had the Palestinians not walked away from those offers in 2000 and in 2008, there would today be two peoples settled in their homelands behind secure borders.

Ultimately, sooner or later, all wars and all conflicts end, with a bang or with a whimper. There is no reason to assume that the Israeli-Palestinian conflict is more intractable than others. But *if we have learnt anything over the past 25 years, it is that being ambiguous about the simple fact that neither side is going to have the entirety of the land does no one any favors. Israelis will have to accept the fact that they cannot build settlements all over the West Bank, and Palestinians will have to accept the fact that they cannot settle inside Israel in the name of return.* The sooner both sides hear and internalize these simple, cold, hard truths, the sooner we will be able to speak of hope again

THE GAZA PROTESTS ARE ABOUT ENDING ISRAEL

Op-Ed for Forward, May 2018

In the past few days, we have come closer than we have in some time to touching the core issues that drive the conflict between Israelis, Palestinians, and the wider Arab and Islamic world.

After decades of discussing "territories," "borders," "settlements," "two states" and "occupation," and lamenting the lack of trust between the sides and the absence of leadership, *we are finally discussing the key question, which is: Is the Arab and Islamic world, and the Palestinians among them, ready to acknowledge that the Jewish people, as a people, have the equal right to self-determination and sovereignty in their ancestral homeland?*

Put another way, is Israel a temporary aberration in what should be properly an Arab and Islamic region?

The twin images of the clashes on the 1967 border of Palestinian Gaza with Israel, and the inauguration of the American Embassy in Jerusalem, both serve to highlight the two dominant issues in the conflict that directly touch upon the question of the right of the Jewish people to the land: Jerusalem, and the Palestinian demand for "return" into the state of Israel within its pre 1967 lines.

No other two issues expose so clearly the extent to which the dominant Islamic, Arab and Palestinian narrative remains still one in which Israel is a colonial enterprise of a foreign, invented people who came out of nowhere to a place to which they have no connection.

Jerusalem, or as it is also known, Zion, is the city that gave birth to the modern movement for national liberation of the Jewish people: Zionism. It is the continuous cultural and historical connection of the Jewish people to Zion over millennia, and the history of the Judean sovereign presence there that underpins the claim of the Jewish people to be an indigenous people with a legitimate right to the land.

The denial of that connection of the Jewish people to Zion therefore stands at the heart of the Palestinian, Arab and Islamic denial of the right of the Jewish people to the city, and by extension, to the entirety of the land. It forms the basis for repeated efforts in UNESCO, international bodies, and repeated Palestinians declarations and speeches that refuse to acknowledge the longstanding Jewish connection to the city, and by extension, the Jewish rights to at least some of it.

In parallel, for several weeks, people in Gaza have been marching on its borders with Israel, a march that included armed attacks on the border, with the declared intent of marching into Israel and exercising what the Palestinians consider their absolute and superior "Right of Return."

While many of the west, in a manner typical of a phenomenon I have come to term Westplaining, have explained away the Palestinian statement about "return" and "taking back" Israel as expressions of anger at the deteriorating conditions in Gaza and the maritime blockade, the Palestinians have not marched for any of these issues. If they had, they would have stormed the Gaza border with Egypt.

The Palestinians were very clear: What they demand is "return."

The Palestinian demand for "return" has been shaped in the wake of the 1949 failure to prevent the establishment of the state of Israel. Having failed to prevent the UN partition vote diplomatically, and having failed to prevent Israel's emergence militarily, the demand for "return" was shaped as a continuation of the war against Israel by other means, a war that continues to this day.

It is precisely the reason why *despite Israel retreating fully to the 1967 lines between Gaza and Israel, the people of Gaza are demanding to take what is beyond those lines, which they still believe is very much theirs.*

If the war is ever to end with true peace, the Palestinians as well as the Arab and Islamic world at large have to come to accept the Jewish people as an indigenous people who have come home and who have an equal and legitimate right to their ancestral land.

As much as it seems counterintuitive, peace becomes more possible to achieve the more it becomes clear that the "hope" of Israel's temporariness is a costly delusion. This is the core issue, and the closer we come to touching it, with all the pain it entails, the closer we will come to peace.

HOW UNRWA PREVENTS GAZA THRIVING

Op-Ed Co-Authored with Adi Schwartz for Haaretz, June 2018

It's the same old tune – renewed discussion about "reconstructing and redeveloping" the Gaza Strip. Again people are talking about some kind of "arrangement" for managing Gaza's reconstruction, whether under Egyptian, Qatari or American auspices. There's more talk of huge investments in a port and in water and power infrastructures, and about creating jobs.

Wasted efforts, all. They're doomed to fail, the same as all the other reconstruction attempts in recent years. As long as the political landmine at the heart of the matter – the perpetuation of the status of Gaza's residents as refugees from "Palestine" – is not defused, there's no real possibility for rebuilding and developing the Gaza Strip.

The problem is that Gaza's inhabitants do not view that piece of land as their home, but rather as a transit camp they will inhabit until the day they can return to what they believe is their home. Because of this, they will far prefer to invest their efforts and resources in returning to their "true" home – by force if necessary – than in cultivating the temporary one where they currently reside.

Of the 1.8 million people living in Gaza, 1.3 million are registered as refugees with the United Nations Relief and Works Agency for Palestine Refugees (UNRWA). In other words, three-quarters of the people in the Strip possess a status that is by definition temporary in character – one granted to someone who is between permanent residence in one locale and permanent habitation in a second place.

When UNRWA was established, in the wake of the 1947-1949 war, it spent its first few years in an earnest effort to assist the Arab refugees from the war (the Jewish ones were taken care of by the newly established State of Israel) in rebuilding their lives in their new locations, whether in the West Bank and Gaza,

Jordan, Lebanon or Syria. But within a few short years, it became painfully clear that neither the Palestinians themselves, nor the Arab host countries were willing to let this process take place, as it would legitimize the outcome of the war in the form of the establishment of the State of Israel.

Having failed to prevent the vote on partition in the UN General Assembly, or prevent partition itself and the birth of Israel through war and military invasions, the Palestinians and the Arab host states mobilized to turn the demand for "return" to Israel into one of the central means by which the outcome of the war, in the form of a sovereign state for the Jewish people, could be undone. To that end, UNRWA then was taken over by the Palestinians, becoming an organization that would grant them the official status of "refugees" until that day of "return."

These 1.3 million refugees, some of whom are the fifth generation of Palestinian families who arrived in the Strip in 1948, long for the moment when they will be able to return to their ancestral homes (most of which do not exist anymore) in Ashdod, Ashkelon and Be'er Sheva, and believe that this moment is possible and close at hand. Their dream – and that of their brethren in the West Bank, Jordan, Lebanon and Syria – has coalesced into a collective demand whose import was and continues to be a continuing war on Israel by other means. Clinging to the dream of return makes it possible for the Palestinians not to accept the consequences of their defeat, and to believe that even if they lost a few battles, the overall war against Zionism still isn't over.

Still, there's a tangible difference between dreams and the demands that are nurtured by international support under UN sanction. The State of Israel cannot exert a direct influence on the Palestinian dream of return, but it can definitely act to deny the dream the fuel that sustains it, and that fuel comes from the West.

Under the influence of various interests in the Arab world, the international community became complicit in the process of leaving so many Palestinians in a legal, social and economic limbo, awaiting "return." The West in particular, providing the bulk of the funds for UNRWA's operations, unwittingly became the central source of sustenance for the Palestinian idea that it is better to continue to struggle for "return" rather than come to terms with the legitimacy of Israel and build a new life of prosperity in the West Bank and Gaza.

This has to change. Israel can and should intervene with UNRWA's donor countries – the United States, Australia, Britain and the European Union – and insist that they cease and desist from supporting the Palestinian demand to annihilate Israel, by way of their support for UNRWA. Countries that officially support the two-state solution cannot underwrite an organization whose aim is to ensure that the Jewish people, as a people, will not have a sovereign state.

UNRWA's essence involves making it clear to the more than 70 percent of Gaza inhabitants registered as refugees, that Gaza is not their true home. It does so by providing the political infrastructure that grants Palestinians the status of "refugees," which they would not otherwise merit if international standards were applied to them; by passing this status on to their descendants automatically and in perpetuity, while opposing any effort to find solutions for those registered as "refugees," other than in the context of the collective demand for "return." It is this that UNRWA often refers to by the code words "just solution" and "legitimate rights," of which it calls itself the protector. UNRWA makes it clear to the "refugees" in Gaza (and in all of its other areas of operations) that their "true home," wrested from them by force, lies across the border. People who grow up with that belief will assuredly use cement, when given it, not to build permanent homes, but to dig tunnels to the place which, as far as they are concerned, is their real home.

It is not only parents and grandparents who cultivate this

dream. Every day, residents go into the streets of Gaza and see UNRWA signs on the schools and clinics that the organization operates. They read those signs to mean that the UN – that is, the world community – recognizes them as refugees and encourages their "return" to Israel.

The chances of reconstructing and developing the Gaza Strip will be greater without UNRWA, and even if some benefit accrues to cooperation with the UN organization in Gaza, it is far outweighed by the damage the agency has wrought. Ever since 1967, when Israel's security establishment chose to cooperate with UNRWA and enable its ongoing operations in the West Bank and Gaza, it has argued that UNRWA is a moderating force, without whose education and healthcare services greater violence would prevail. But given that in Gaza and Lebanon, where UNRWA's operations are most extensive, and the ratio of Palestinians served by UNRWA who still live in refugee camps is the greatest (50 percent as compared to 25 percent in the West Bank, and 18 percent in Jordan) – the time has come to ask how many Israeli soldiers and civilians have been killed in the rounds of fighting in Gaza and Lebanon because of the extreme terrorist elements that the refugee-camp culture there has spawned.

Israel has declared preventing aggravation of the situation in Gaza as a security interest, and it still operates on the assumption that it is not possible to aid the Strip without UNRWA, which is helping to prevent a humanitarian disaster there. Indeed, because UNRWA has succeeded in concealing its political raison d'etre of sustaining the Palestinian demand for "return" designed to undo Israel, and it has done so under a humanitarian guise – it enjoys cooperation from Israel as well as international funding. In Gaza the organization has also become, in good part thanks to Israel, the principal conduit for the international aid that is supposed to be used to rebuild the Gaza Strip.

That is a mistake: UNRWA cannot be a true and sincere partner in Gaza's reconstruction. On the contrary: The fact that UNRWA is a major actor in the attempts to rebuild Gaza plays a decisive part in the repeated failure of those efforts.

Perhaps Israel cannot take away the Palestinians' dream to return to Ashkelon, Ashdod and Be'er Sheva, but at the very least it can and should take action to terminate international support for the agency that stokes that dream. As such, it is necessary first and foremost to recognize the fact that the damage caused to Israel by UNRWA's continued existence dwarfs any tactical advantage it may offer.

No place for cooperation

It is possible, however, to preserve Israel's security interests while aiding in the development of Gaza and preventing further deterioration of living conditions and growing extremism.

First, Israel must demand that every international move to rebuild and develop the Gaza Strip be accompanied by clear declarations on the part of the donor countries, certainly the Western ones, that they do not recognize the claim that the residents of Gaza are refugees from Palestine. On the contrary, *Israel must demand that the donor countries assert that, because Gaza is part of Palestine, and because Israel has no territorial claims on it – all residents of Gaza are Palestinian Gazans and they have no right to make claims to the sovereign territory of the State of Israel, or demand "return" by virtue of their being registered as "refugees" from Palestine. They already live in Palestine.*

It is time to tell the Palestinians loud and clear: There is no "right" of "return" and there never will be. The future of the Gazans is in Gaza. There will be no Arab Palestine from the sea to the river. There can be an Arab Palestine in Gaza and the West Bank, but certainly not one that supersedes Israel. In fact, the price of a Palestinian state in the West Bank and Gaza is forgoing any claims to an Arab Palestine in the rest of the territory where Israel exists.

Second, Israel itself must announce the termination of its voluntary cooperation with UNRWA in the Gaza Strip. The fact that Israel did cooperate for so long stems from decades of short-sightedness, during which such cooperation seemed to be providing quiet. But that "quiet" was ultimately bought at a bloody cost, due to the conflict's prolongation and exacerbation.

If an arrangement becomes possible in which the Palestinian Authority is once more the main administrative factor in Gaza, it can become the principal channel for aid. The countries that donate to UNRWA will be able to transfer the hundreds of millions of dollars they now give to UNRWA annually directly to the PA to benefit UNRWA hospitals and schools. Nothing will change in terms of the actual provision of services – only the sign outside the buildings. The UNRWA school will become the school of the PA, but students, teachers and curriculum will remain the same. Likewise for the hospitals. The Palestinians are likely to continue teaching in those schools that all of Palestine is exclusively theirs, but they would no longer do so under the aegis of the UN.

Such steps will show that Israel does not object to the services being provided in a manner that helps build an infrastructure for a functioning Palestinian state, but does object to their provision through an organization that is actively preserving the dream of Israel's destruction.

If the PA is unable to operate in Gaza, aid should be transferred through a new and apolitical umbrella organization whose only purpose would be the reconstruction and development of the Strip. Israel would declare its willingness to take far-reaching actions on behalf of this effort, but make them conditional on the establishment of the new organization and transfer of all of UNRWA's activity to this organization, whose operations would not involve granting refugee status to its clients.

If the United Nations is capable of acting instantaneously to dispatch rescue operations to disaster areas around the world, and to assist earthquake victims in Haiti or tsunami victims in Southeast Asia without necessarily classifying them as refugees, it is also capable of doing so in Gaza.

Another possibility is for the Western donor countries to act in conjunction with other humanitarian organizations already operating in Gaza, such as USAID, UNICEF and others. Every one of these groups is preferable to UNRWA, because UNRWA links the humanitarian aid that Gaza needs to its own political support for the idea of "return," and this only precludes the possibility of any future conciliation between the peoples.

The rebuilding process must be based on the simple insight that those who live in the Gaza Strip will themselves invest their efforts and resources in the Strip only if they believe that their future lies there. Therefore, it is out of the question to entrust rebuilding efforts to those who are subverting that message. It's not by chance that over time, significantly larger sums per capita have been funneled into the efforts to develop Gaza and into UNRWA than went into the Marshall Plan. *As long as the ostensible reconstruction efforts are implemented by those who do not truly wish to build a new future for the residents in question, this will be a bottomless pit.*

Only a decision to stop fuelling the idea of return completely will create a true chance to rehabilitate Gaza so that its inhabitants will transform it into a worthy place, and in the long run perhaps achieve something else: coming to terms with the legitimacy of the State of Israel as the sovereign state of the Jewish people, on the path to peace.

LET'S LAY THE MYTH TO REST: RABIN WOULD NOT HAVE BROUGHT PEACE

Op-Ed for Forward, November 2020

There is a reigning myth that when Yigal Amir assassinated Israeli Prime Minister Yitzhak Rabin on November 4, 1995, he also assassinated peace. It is, like many myths, at once comforting and entirely wrong.

This myth is comforting because it reinforces the kind of foundational story that Western civilization is based on, from Christ to the modern superhero. In these stories, a savior figure or leader shapes history through sheer force of will and against all odds. Transplanted to the Middle East, this foundational myth sets the stage by casting peace between Israelis and Palestinians as requiring an end-of-times salvation. And Yitzhak Rabin is the savior who could have brought about salvation and peace on earth had he not been martyred.

But this myth also reinforces another foundational Western trope, in which Jews are always cast as having an outsized role in shaping human affairs. This is why Jewish agency is always elevated over Palestinian agency in the context of the Middle East. Had Rabin been alive there would have been peace, the myth goes, and since Rabin was assassinated by a Jew, there is no peace. Thanks to the addition of the Jewish trope, the actions, goals and world view of Palestinians have no bearing on the possibility or impossibility of the attainment of peace.

But the reason to be suspicious of the myth of the Rabin assassination killing peace is not just because of how neatly it fits into the wishful thinking of Western storytelling. The myth has persisted for another reason, too: because it rests on the belief that we cannot know what would have happened had he lived.

But we actually do: When he died, Rabin was already on his

way to being trounced in direct elections by the up and coming **Benjamin Netanyahu**. Rabin was going to lose because there was a cavernous gulf between the handshakes on manicured lawns following elevated speeches about peace on the one hand, and the bloody massacres carried out by Palestinian suicide bombers against Israeli civilians on the other. And this gulf did not endear Israelis to the cause of peace. In the highly unlikely case that Rabin would have won the elections, the Israeli public would have pressured him to put the brakes on the so-called peace process, and there is evidence that he was already planning to do so.

Moreover, the shock of the assassination actually swung Israelis to the left, nearly preventing what was a secure Netanyahu victory. Israelis swung so much to the left that a few short years later, **Ehud Barak was elected** on a platform for peace more far reaching than anything imagined by Rabin. Ehud Barak **said yes to the Clinton Parameters** that would have created an independent Palestinian state in the West Bank and Gaza, with its capital in east Jerusalem, including the Old City. It was Arafat who walked away from this opportunity with no criticism from his people.

If Arafat walked away from a proposal that was far more ambitious than anything Rabin would have put on the table, what reason is there to believe that Rabin would have brought peace?

It brings us back to that phantom, Palestinian agency. Palestinians are agents of history no more and no less than all other human beings. As such, they have made it clear in the past century that if the price of Palestinian independence is the establishment of a Jewish state in the other part of the land, they are not interested. It is a goal that the Palestinian leadership has pursued consistently, as agents of history do.

Twenty-five years after Rabin's assassination, it's time to part with comforting but erroneous myths. Rabin was a human, Israeli leader who tried to make peace and would have failed, as did Barak and Olmert after him. He ultimately represented the Zionist idea, with which Palestinians are still at war.

Leaders, elected or not, cannot stray much from the foundational ethos of their people and survive. Israelis and Palestinians will only make peace when one of two things happen: Either Jews, as a people, will forgo their commitment to Zionism, or Palestinians, as a people, will forgo their war against Zionism.

When one of these two things happen, hopefully the second, the leaders who reflect this change will make themselves known.

THE REAL KILLER OF THE TWO STATE SOLUTION

Op-Ed for Forward, July 2020

Twenty years ago, in July 2000, we were filled with hope as Ehud Barak, Israel's Prime Minister and leader of the Labor Party, left for Camp David to negotiate a final peace agreement with the Palestinians. After more than a decade of previously unimaginable historical breakthroughs – the collapse of the Soviet Union, the fall of the Berlin Wall, the end of Apartheid in South Africa and the Good Friday Agreement in Northern Ireland – we believed we had arrived at the historical moment when peace with the Palestinians might finally be at hand.

Barak placed a bold proposal on the negotiating table that would have provided the Palestinians with an independent sovereign state in almost all of the West Bank and Gaza, without a single settlement in sight, and a capital in east Jerusalem, including holy sites. And we were certain the Palestinians would say yes. After all, for decades we had been told that the key to peace in the Middle East was for Israel to hand over land – "land for peace" – and Barak had just agreed to hand over the land to the Palestinians.

Moreover, **we made the straightforward assumption that when a people who seek to govern themselves in their own state are presented with the opportunity to do so, they say yes. We were wrong.**

There was no yes. Yasser Arafat, the leader of the Palestine Liberation Organization, walked away. He walked away from Barak's proposal at Camp David, and he walked away from President Clinton's proposal which set the parameters for peace. Had he not walked away, the state of Palestine would have celebrated twenty years of independence this year, in its capital in Jerusalem.

So why did he walk away? Why did Arafat not say a resounding yes when presented with the opportunity to give his people the

126

liberty and dignity of political independence? And why did he face no criticism whatsoever from his people for doing so? **What did the Palestinians actually want if not an independent state in the West Bank and Gaza with its capital in east Jerusalem?**

The answer was hiding in plain sight: the right of return.

The overriding Palestinian demand, more important than the explicit demand of statehood, has always been the innocuous sounding right of return — the demand for millions of Palestinians, descendants of those who fled or were expelled in the 1948 war, to be recognized as possessing each a "right" to settle inside the state of Israel. This right, not sanctioned by international law, crucially overrules Israeli sovereignty; since the number of these Palestinians is between five and nine million, and since Israel's Jewish population is about seven million, the meaning of such a demand is the transformation of Israel into an Arab state.

And this demand for a massive collective right to enter Israel has been inseparable from the larger negotiations from the Palestinian side. What this means is that when Arafat and Mahmoud Abbas, the head of the Palestinian Authority, spoke of their support for a two-state solution, they actually envisioned two Arab states: one in the West Bank and Gaza, and another one to replace Israel.

This is the only two-state solution Palestinians have ever agreed to. **There has never been a Palestinian vision of peace where the sovereign state of the Jewish people is allowed to remain as is, because there has never been a Palestinian vision that didn't include the right of return for millions of Palestinians.**

This is why Arafat walked away in 2000. "Recognition of the right of return," said an internal PLO memo written a short time after the Camp David summit, "is a prerequisite for the closure of the conflict." The same week, an official magazine of Arafat's faction within the PLO wrote that the mass return of Palestinian refugees to Israel would "help Jews get rid of racist Zionism."

Eight years later, When Secretary of State Condoleezza Rice sketched out the details of Israeli Prime Minister Ehud Olmert's peace proposal to Abbas in May 2008, his telling response, quoted in her memoir "No Higher Honor," was, "I can't tell four million Palestinian [refugees] that only five thousand of them can go home."

And as in 2000, there was no criticism of Abbas for depriving Palestinians of a state, no Op-Eds saying that this was a great opportunity that should have been grabbed with both hands, and no NGOs calling on Palestinians to move on from the fixation on return.

One thing Abbas might have told these Palestinian refugees was that the twentieth century saw many empires collapsing and nation-states established, often in a bloody and painful process of land division and border drawings that caused the death and displacement of tens of millions of human beings. Many of them, just like the Palestinians, wanted to return to the places where they had lived before. But it was only the Palestinian demand to resettle inside the State of Israel that was indulged and sustained in such a way by the international community. The fact is, no other refugee population exists from the 1940s. They have all moved on to build their lives in the places to which they fled or in other countries.

The refusal on the part of the international community to engage these simple truths is telling. *In 1947, British Foreign Minister Ernst Bevin summarized the essence of the conflict in the British Mandate territory as boiling down to the fact that the Jews want a state in the land, and the Arabs want the Jews not to have a state in the land. He has only been proven right ever since.* More than the Palestinians wanted a state for themselves, they still want the Jewish people not to have their own state in the land, in any borders.

And as long as the price of having a Palestinian Arab state in the land was going to be that the Jewish people would have their own state in the land as well, the answer was going to be no, no and — to quote Abu Mazen — "a thousand times no."

The Palestine Liberation Organization did undergo a shift at the end of the 1980s. The collapse of the Soviet Union, the PLO's military, diplomatic and economic patron for decades, forced the Palestinian organization to look for support in the West. That in turn forced the PLO to change its tone, while not its core position: the total rejection of the State of Israel. Gone were the days of the revolutionary violent rhetoric; the need to solve the conflict in peaceful means came to the front.

But this was only tactical, and has not as yet done anything to put a dent in the maximalist vision of Arab rule over the entire land manifested in the demand for a "right of return," which has never been taken off the table, and to which the goal of two-states was always subordinate.

Further evidence for how much the Palestinian leadership was willing to sacrifice the two-state solution to the right of return came in 2011, when some 1,700 original documents were leaked from the office of chief Palestinian negotiator Saeb Erekat and published online by Al Jazeera. The documents, known as the Palestine Papers, were internal PA memos and other papers, which document a decade of peace negotiations with Israel.

The papers reveal that the Palestinian leadership was so serious about the "right of return" that they were unwilling to countenance phrases and formulations that might jeopardize it – including "two states for two peoples," which was viewed as a threat to the realization of the demand to return. In a memorandum for Saeb Erekat on May 3, 2009, for example, the negotiating team writes, "Reference to the right of the two peoples to self-determination in two states may have an adverse impact on refugee rights, namely the right of return... Further, a recognition of the principle of two states for two peoples as a solution to the Israeli-Palestinian conflict confirms that the PLO no longer envisages Palestinian self-determination within the territory of the state of Israel."

In another memorandum dated November 2007, the Palestinian negotiating team explained that recognizing Israel as a Jewish state "would likely be treated as ... an implicit waiver of the right of return" and "would undermine the legal rights of the refugees."

Another document from June 2008, which makes recommendations on the refugee issue, notes that the formulation "'two states for two peoples' implies no return... to Israel." And a document from May 2009 states that as far as refugee rights and Israel's responsibility for the creation of the Palestinian refugee problem, "referring to 'two states for two peoples' embodies similar risks to those associated with the recognition of Israel as the state of the Jewish people."

These documents reveal not just efforts to undermine the two-state solution; they reveal that it was never an option in the first place. One hears a lot these days about the death of the two-state solution. Israel, we are told, killed it off with settlement expansion. Or it was the U.S. who killed it by moving the embassy to Jerusalem.

The truth is, the two-state solution was never killed — not by Israel or the U.S. — because in the Palestinian vision, it was never conceived. Jews and Arabs have the right to live in freedom and dignity, and to possess the political power to secure both their individual and collective rights. But for that to happen, the biggest obstacle must be recognized right now and addressed upfront.

The demand of massive Palestinian entry into Israel, uniquely indulged by the west for generations, should be rejected. As long as Palestinians reject the equal right of the Jewish people to political power and self-governance in any part of the land and seek to undo it through "return," no political solution will bring peace.

THERE IS NO SILENCE TO BE BROKEN ON THE OCCUPATION

Book Review for the Tel Aviv Review of Books, Spring 2022

The publication of the book *Who Do You Think You Are?* by Yuli Novak is evidence, once more, that the artistic bar for anti-Zionist creation is low. The book is badly written. The metaphors worn out. Descriptions of nature as stand-ins for emotional turmoil (comparing volcanic eruptions to her turmoil, geological changes to social ones, comparing getting lost and found while traveling to getting lost and found emotionally), present throughout, would barely cut it as a high school writing exercise. But because the book tells the story of how Zionism is so irredeemable that it must be scrapped altogether, the low literary value of the book is ignored. Given that the book peddles a recent incarnation of the ancient idea that no amount of reform could make the collective Jew palatable, there is a thriving and stable market for material that caters to it.

Who Do You Think You Are? is part biography, part political reflection, part coming-of-age story. Unfortunately, though, there is no coming of age. The protagonist begins and ends the story as the same petulant child whose so-called reflections lead her to realize that the world is to blame, and everyone but her is "blind, numb, fearful and angry." A vein of irresponsibility runs through the book. The protagonist just happens to do things. By her own description, Novak became director of **Breaking the Silence**, an organization devoted to ending Israel's military occupation of the West Bank, on a lark. She was studying to be a lawyer but didn't want to be one and hadn't yet figured out what she wanted to do. She came across a job ad for director of Breaking the Silence and thought it was "something worth trying." Why? Not clear.

Once at the job she doesn't understand why people get angry. Israeli Jews who respond to Palestinian attacks with "hysteria" and are manipulated by politicians into "fear and hatred" are at fault. She and her colleagues merely want to highlight the "inherent immorality" of the Occupation. The fury against her is because she "stood up against the regime." The forces that oppose her are nefarious and anti-democratic. They target Breaking the Silence to promote an "illiberal order" and "concentration of powers by the government."

Her intentions have always been nothing but good. Oh, and the media is at fault.

Theoretically, bad writing and childish protagonists could still make smart arguments. Alas, not in this book. Even if judging only on substance, each of the author's premises is wrong. The first is that Jewish citizens of Israel do not know what is involved in exercising military control over Palestinians in the West Bank, the Occupation. If they knew, they would end it. Therefore, there is a need to "break the silence" surrounding the Occupation. This is a tantalizing idea. It appeals to the human desire to uncover dark secrets lurking beneath the surface. It lures people with the promise that they will hear something they have not heard before. It also confers a halo of martyrdom on those willing to break the so-called silence.

If only. *The last thing surrounding Israel's military control of the West Bank since 1967 is silence. From the moment Israel's military has come to control the West Bank area captured from the Kingdom of Jordan, following King Hussein's ill-fated decision to follow the charismatic Nasser into that disastrous war, there has been nothing but noise about it. Articles, interviews, reports, commentaries, documentaries, photos, video footage, movies, political debates, UN resolutions, international pronouncements, NGOs, movements, posts, tweets, memes. Jews, Arabs, Muslim, Israelis, Palestinians, Westerners, non-Westerners, academics, celebrities. All weighed in. Perhaps in a small village in China there is a person who has not had something to say about Israel's Occupation of the West Bank. There is no silence to be broken.*

The Occupation does not take place in a distant location. Israelis encounter it in numerous ways, not least of which is service in the military. Almost all of Israel's non-Haredi Jewish citizens serve in the military. Almost all of those who serve or have served in Israel's military had to contribute to maintaining that military control, from intelligence gathering to incarceration to boots on the ground. Israelis who serve in the military talk. Israeli Jews, (and Arabs), are not known for their reticence in use of words. Israelis know what is involved in maintaining the Occupation. Israeli ignorance is not the problem. The first and major premise of *Who Do You Think You Are?* and of the entire efforts of Breaking the Silence's effort is that "what allows the Occupation to persist is the public silence around how it's carried out and its ethical and moral implications." This, by virtue of simple observation, is wrong.

Well then, if Israelis know about the Occupation and what is involved in its maintenance, and there is no need to break a non-existing silence around it, why do don't they just end it? And "if not now," when are they going to end it? According to the "political rationale" of Breaking the Silence, as explained by Novak, a straight line goes from Israelis hearing the stories of soldiers serving in the West Bank to realizing the "inherent immorality" of the Occupation and wanting to end it. There are two binary alternatives: the immoral choice of continuing the Occupation or the moral choice of ending it.

Like her colleagues across the Atlantic at **If Not Now**, an American organization nominally calling for ending Israel's military occupation, Novak wants Israel to "just end the occupation." Sure, how? Unfortunately, missing from the entire book is any serious consideration of policy alternatives and their attendant risks. Could it just be that, given all the bad choices, Israeli Jews understand that maintaining the Occupation is a dirty business, but rationally consider it (oh, the horror) the least bad of their real-world alternatives? But no, not for Novak this worldly business of choosing among several bad real-world alternatives. Presenting choices that are not black and white, good and evil, moral and immoral seems to be outside Novak's interests. Whether ideas like Goodman's "reduction of conflict" or decoupling the necessity of the military occupation as long as the Palestinian war with the state of Israel continues, from the question of unnecessary settlements, which this author champions, is not even discussed. Most problematic, the possibility that, despite multiple efforts, Israel has not been able to end its military control of the West Bank through an agreement is because Palestinians refuse to sign any agreement that is not effectively "From the River to the Sea" is never even considered.

Novak continues a long tradition of viewing the conflict through the prism of Jewish agency and Palestinian passivity. Jews are perpetrators. Palestinians are victims. Jews act. Palestinians respond. Jews provoke. Palestinians are provoked. The notion that Palestinians carry out deliberate acts against Jews in Israel to realize a clearly articulated vision of "From the River to the Sea" is nowhere to be found, except, ironically, in Palestinian expressions, available everywhere, except in Novak's book. *Who Do You Think You Are?* partakes in this neo-colonial vision that deprives Palestinians of agency. The entire conversation takes place in the author's head between different Israeli points of view. Worse, the entire book centers around the author's feelings about morality. She felt "Breaking the Silence" was the moral thing to do. And then "it didn't' work out anymore," "it was too difficult," "it was in my head," "something was broken inside me and I didn't know what," "I couldn't anymore," "It was too much responsibility," "too much fear," "too much loneliness." It just didn't "feel" right.

To Novak, everything is binary. She believed lies. Now she knows the truth. Zionists favor the state. She favors the individual. There is nothing in between. No nuance. No sophistication of thought. She was part of a matrix of Zionism that could only be sustained by "denial and avoidance." Now she clearly sees that it is a "lie" that a sovereign Jewish state could exist without the Occupation. Why? She just feels it. When Novak fought "only" against the Occupation and not against Jewish self-determination altogether she was part of the system, and she bears responsibility for its "inherent immorality." Novak mindlessly adopts fashionable ideas about whiteness and colonialism that could only take place when one is deprived of any historical understanding of the Jewish people. She claims Israel is not like South Africa only to immediately make that comparison. Novak's ahistorical attitude is obvious throughout as she speaks of fighting the occupation because it's happening "now" and who cares how we got here.

The desire for moral purity and resolution of the "inherent contradictions of Zionism" is another aspect of the petulance of the protagonist. It is a desire, present as much among Western Jews as among some Israeli Jews of the left, to achieve moral purity through powerlessness. It is the Jewish idea that my colleague Shany Mor calls "the last time Jews behaved morally was at the lines to the gas showers at Auschwitz." It is a desire to free the Jewish soul from the Jewish body. To forgo the messy moral earthy life of Zionism for the moral purity of Jewish powerlessness. For some Jews, like Novak, the "inherent contradiction" they cannot sustain is not left-wing Zionism or even Zionism itself, but the very idea of Jewish power. What Novak seeks is "rebirth on a different soil."

Novak travels around the world, clearly running away from something. Towards the end of the book her answer is that she ran away from coming to terms with the fact that she could no longer be a Zionist. She struggled because she couldn't know who she is without Zionism. It is a supremely self-centered position. The most important thing for Novak is to feel good about who she is, everyone else be damned. In Novak's world there is no history and there are no others. It is all about her, how she feels, and what is happening now.

By the end of the book Novak has left behind her earthy Zionism with all its contradictions. Like a spiritual born-again she is ready to embrace some vague utopia of individual equality and democracy unmoored from any sense of history and people. Like many utopians before her Novak is very good at the noble task of destroying what exists and clueless at building something new. There is probably no more anti-Zionist mindset, not in the sense of being opposed to Zionism, but in negating its very spirit. The genius of Zionism was that it had a vision for building something and went about realizing it. Zionism didn't just tear down, although its thinkers had plenty of harsh criticism, not least of which about Jewish life in the diaspora. Zionism was very specific about what it sought to build and how it planned to go about building it and had the ruthless determination that came with it.

From inception, Zionism had thoughtful and fierce detractors who mounted thoughtful critiques. With Novak, we now have soft naval gazers whose only concern is how anything makes them feel. One could only be nostalgic for the days when Zionism had more formidable foes...

PALESTINIAN REFUGEE 'RETURN': CRITIQUE

Essay Co-Authored with Adi Schwartz for Fathom Journal, June 2021

Peter Beinart is close. He is slowly inching towards understanding the core of the conflict. He finally realises that the conflict is clearly not about all those things that we were told for decades. It is not about the military occupation of lands controlled as a result of the 1967 war. It is not about the settlements built in those lands. It is not even about Israeli control of East Jerusalem. While obviously Palestinian Arabs want all of these to end, Beinart understands that ending those would not bring an end to the conflict. Perhaps having read our book *The War of Return*, as he describes (*The Guardian*, May 18), Beinart finally understands that Palestinians have always wanted something more. *He understands that the Palestinian demand to settle inside the sovereign territory of the state of Israel in the name of 'return' — known as 'The Right of Return' — is far more important to Palestinians than those issues related to the 'occupation', 'settlements', and even Jerusalem.*

So Beinart proposes that Israel accept that demand to settle millions of Palestinians inside Israel, arguing that it is both doable, desirable, and above all — a deep realisation of Jewish values. Doing so, he believes, would redress decades-old Palestinian grievances, which would in turn allow peace and prosperity to prevail.

But Beinart's proposal misses entirely what the 'Right of Return' was designed to achieve. As we discuss in depth in our book, *this idea of a 'Right' of all Palestinians to settle en masse in Israel, in breach of its sovereignty, which was never recognised as a right under international law, was developed by the Arabs after their defeat in the war of 1948, purposefully as a means of continuing that war by other means.* Demanding 'return' was never meant to achieve peace, but to obtain the same goal that escaped the Arabs in the war of 1948 — the prevention of Jewish self-determination.

Settling the original refugees and their millions of descendants in the State of Israel was not, and is still not, a humanitarian gesture, as Beinart seems to believe, but a political action, aimed at restoring Arab and Muslim dominance to a land that the Palestinians view as exclusively theirs. In that, the 'Right of Return" was never an innocent idea, divorced from the broader Arab political rejection of Jewish self-determination. It was never about simply returning Arabs to the entirety of the land — but about returning the entirety of the land to the Arabs.

This is the reason why, despite many Palestinian refugees wanting to return to their homes in the course of the war or immediately thereafter, the Palestinian leadership opposed it, arguing that doing so at that particular moment would mean effective recognition of Israel's existence. It was clear that the issue of the return of the refugees was subsidiary to the greater question of denying Israel's legitimacy. As long as the refugees' return was considered to reflect favorably on Israel's legitimacy, it was rejected. In the summer of 1948, the Jerusalem Mufti Haj Amin al-Husseini, the leader of the Palestinian Arabs, signed a decree in the name of the Arab Higher Committee, assailing the willingness of Arab states to return the refugees to Israel on the grounds that this would require negotiations with the newborn state and would thus grant it effective recognition and legitimacy.

In the same spirit, another Arab Higher Committee official, Emil Ghury, rejected any possibility of returning the refugees home, since this would 'serve as the first step towards Arab recognition of the State of Israel and of partition.' The solution, in his words, 'was only possible through the renewed conquest of the territory that was captured by the Jews and the return of its inhabitants.' The return was part and parcel of the reconquest of the territory. He explicitly warned against seeing the problem through too small a lens, as if it were a purely humanitarian question. He lamented that 'they have turned a matter of *jihad* into a problem of refugees. Looking to the future, Ghury was clear, resolving: 'We are concerned to return and turn the question into a question of *jihad*. We are concerned to harvest hatred of the Jews in the heart of every Arab.'

This was the beginning of a linkage that exists to this day between the refugee problem and the broader aims of the Arab world in the conflict. Palestinian leaders demonstrated that they considered the plight of the refugees secondary to the main political question—the elimination of Israel, the reversal of the outcome of the war, and the prevention of territorial partition. Return, therefore, was not and is still not, merely a matter of geography, but also of time. It is not merely about moving ten or twenty miles to homes left behind, but primarily about returning to a time before the establishment of Israel and The Disaster, *The Nakba.* At the time, the disaster was meant to refer not just to the displacement Palestinian Arabs, but to humiliating experience of defeat to the Jews. In the Arab conception, then, 'Return' is not only about physically moving from one place to another but about reversing all prior events.

The Palestinian historian Walid Khalidi elaborated in the 1950s that return was not an end in itself. In words that sound like a direct response to Beinart's misguided aspirations, he wrote: 'It is sometimes suggested that the way to solve the Palestine problem is to approach it in a piecemeal fashion . . . Settle the refugees and the biggest obstacle to the solution will be removed. But the Palestine problem will remain as acute as ever with every Palestine refugee settled. The refugees may be the outward evidence of the crime which must be tidied out of sight but nothing will remove the scar of Palestine from Arab hearts ... The solution to the Palestine problem cannot be found in the settlement of the refugees. This admission is the heart of the matter: instead of being a legal or humanitarian issue, then and now, the refugee problem is first and foremost a political problem, reflecting the Arab desire to dominate the entire land and to deny Jews sovereignty in any part of it whatsoever.

Shortly after the war, as the consequences of it became more evident and Israel's establishment more difficult to ignore, the Palestinian leadership radically changed its position. Palestinian leaders realised that demanding refugee return could actually upset the new status quo and undermine the existence of the state of Israel. The demand for return, wrote Palestinian historian Rashid Khalidi in analysing the Arab mood of the time, 'was clearly premised on the liberation of Palestine, i.e., the dissolution of Israel.'

Some Arab politicians and media explicitly linked the demand for return to the elimination of the state of Israel. In October 1949 Egyptian foreign minister Muhammad Salah al-Din said, 'It is well known and understood that the Arabs, in demanding the return of the refugees to Palestine, mean their return as masters of the Homeland and not as its slaves. With greater clarity, they mean the liquidation of the State of Israel'. The Palestinian journalist and historian Nasir al-Din Nashashibi also explained, 'We do not want to return with the flag of Israel flying on a single square metre of our country, and if indeed we wish to return, this is an honoured and honourable return and not a degrading return, not a return that will make us citizens in the State of Israel'.

An article in the Lebanese weekly newspaper *Al-Sayyad* declared in February 1949, as the war ended: 'We are unable to return [the refugees] honorably. Let us therefore try to make them a fifth column in the struggle yet before us. One year later, an article in the same newspaper claimed that the Palestinians' return would 'create a large Arab majority that would serve as the most effective means of reviving the Arab character to Palestine while forming a powerful fifth column for the day of revenge and reckoning'.

'Having lost the war,' wrote historian Avi Shlaim, 'Arab governments used whatever weapons they could find to continue the struggle against Israel, and the refugee problem was a particularly effective weapon for putting Israel on the defensive in the court of international public opinion'. As Benny Morris wrote, 'the refugees had been, and remained, a political problem,' and Arab states reasoned that their return to Israel 'could help undermine the Jewish State, to whose continued existence they objected'.

This is how the Palestinian demand to return was born, and this is the reason for its perpetuation for more than 70 years. Its purpose is to serve the goal of undoing Israel. Therefore, whenever an opportunity arose to solve the humanitarian aspect of the problem, without fulfilling the political goal of Arab dominance in the land, it was rejected. For example, Palestinians rejected Israeli offers to resettle some of the refugees in Israel right after the war as Israeli citizens. They also rejected compensation offers by Israel for the loss of property in the war, if it meant having to sign a comprehensive peace agreement that would legitimise Israel's existence. Even when a Palestinian notable tried to build new houses and livelihoods for the Palestinian refugees in an experimental village in the beginning of the 1950s, thus improving their conditions of life and restoring their human dignity, the Palestinian reaction was to burn down the village. The purpose was not, and still is not, to rectify a moral or humanitarian injustice, as Beinart believes, but to undo Jewish independence. That, in Palestinian and Arab eyes, is the gravest injustice of all — that Jews are sovereign and masters of their fate in an area that Arabs believe should be exclusively theirs.

In January 2001, Fatah's official magazine reiterated this idea arguing that the mass return of refugees would 'help Jews get rid of the racist Zionism that wants to impose their permanent isolation from the rest of the world'. The exercise of the right of return was clearly not about humanitarian issues, but was designed to serve the political purpose of changing Israel's character, terminating its nature as the nation-state of the Jewish people, transforming it into one more Arab-dominated state. In that, the Palestinians were presenting themselves as the kind doctors offering euthanasia for a patient who still very much wishes to live.

This underlying worldview explains why the Nakba is commemorated to this day on May 15th, the day after the establishment of the State of Israel. If the Nakba had meant the memory of Arab Palestinian dispossession or suffering, it could have been marked on the day that Haifa or Jaffa, two of the most important Arab cities prior to the war, fell to Jewish hands. It could have also been observed on the day the village of Deir Yessin was lost — a significant milestone that led to greater Arab flight in the war. But the Nakba does not represent the humanitarian loss of lives, or the fact that some Palestinians became refugees, but the political loss of dominance in any part of the land to the Jews and the humiliating defeat to their forces. *The Nakba therefore continues to this day in Palestinian eyes, not because of possible evictions in Sheikh Jarrah, but because the Nakba is synonymous with the very existence of Israel: it will go on as long as Israel exists, and only Israel's disappearance would put an end to it.* To Palestinians, marking the Nakba is not about memories of the past, but about imagining a future when that past is reversed, Israel is gone and the land in its entirety is Arab.

There is no escaping the simple fact that the conflict persists because the goals of both sides are irreconcilable. Jews want to have a sovereign state in at least part of the land and Palestinian Arabs want for the Jews to not have a sovereign state in any part of the land. As pithily articulated by British Foreign Minister Ernest Bevin on the eve of partition: 'His Majesty's Government have thus been faced with an irreconcilable conflict of principles ... For the Jews the essential point of principle is the creation of a sovereign Jewish State. For the Arabs, the essential point of principle is to resist to the last the establishment of Jewish sovereignty *in any part of Palestine'* (our emphasis). Bevin understood quite well that this was not a conflict between two national movements, each seeking first and foremost its own independence, but rather about one group (the Arabs) seeking first and foremost to foil the independence of another (the Jews). Only a clear choice between these irreconcilable goals could therefore solve the conflict once and for all.

Beinart's answer to this question seems clear: the Jews are the ones who should forfeit their state. This is the long-term project Beinart has been engaging in and to do so he seeks to convince Jews that forfeiting their state and their sovereignty and their self-defense is in fact the true realisation of Jewish values. It is an echo of an ancient dark desire lurking always in Jewish life — to escape the historical weight of being Jewish by disappearing completely, by ceasing to be Jewish, and at the very least by no longer being so visibly and obviously Jewish — as Israel and Zionism so clearly are. At the very least it preserves Jewish morality as a powerless people with no choices, known also as the view that the last time the Jews were truly moral was as they waited to enter the showers at Auschwitz.

In this attempt to portray the dissolution of Jewish sovereignty as a Jewish value Beinart posits an equivalence between Jewish and Palestinian 'return'. But the conceptions of 'return" of each side are merely the reflections of their mutually exclusive goals — of Jewish self-determination versus its denial.

Given that at the birth of Zionism, the vast majority of Jews, having been dispersed for millennia, lived outside the Land of

Israel, self-determination in the land could only be fully realised through Jewish immigration – 'returning' — to the land. Jewish return to the land in of itself was never a goal of Zionism — self-determination was. Jews could return to the Land of Israel, study Torah, live there and be buried for much of their time in exile. That in itself was not a goal of Zionism. The issue was that the land was ruled by others and Jews could not rule themselves. Zionism introduced the possibility that Jews could rule themselves in the land, and to that end called upon them to return to the land and help build their third sovereignty.

Since the premier goal of Zionism was sovereignty in the land rather than return to each and every square metre where their Hebrew, Israelite and Judean ancestors ever stepped, Zionist leaders agreed to various partition plans at every historical juncture. It is not that Jews didn't dream initially of being sovereign in the entire land. The map that Chaim Weizmann presented to the 1919 Paris peace conference included not only the current state of Israel, Judea, Samaria and Gaza, but also parts of today's southern Lebanon and the eastern bank of the River Jordan, today in the Kingdom of Jordan. However, when this plan met with reality, and first and foremost the presence of a large Arab population that resisted Zionist ambitions, Zionism was pragmatic enough to adjust its romantic and spiritual desires to that reality. Since the goal was self-determination, borders were negotiable.

Comparing Weizmann's map with David Ben Gurion's proposal for the partition of the British Mandate in 1946, one can clearly see how pragmatic Zionism was. In this map, submitted by the Jewish Agency to the Anglo-American Committee of Inquiry, one can clearly see the concessions that Zionism made, proposing that an Arab state would be established in the most historic areas of the Holy Land. In some 25 years, Zionism moved from demanding a large piece of the land, to partitioning and settling for what they could reasonably get.

When the United Nations voted in favor of partition in November 1947, it left Jerusalem – Zion in Hebrew, the origin of the word Zionism – in international hands as a corpus separatum. It also left the area known as Judea, just south of Jerusalem – from which the word Jew is derived – in Arab hands. Still, when news broke out that the UN voted in favor of a Jewish state on about half of the territory of the Mandate, thousands of Jews took to the streets and celebrated the coming attainment of sovereignty in even a small part of the land. Even though the Jewish state was to have a substantial Arab population, it was clear that once the state could finally open its doors to Jews from all over the world, the Jewish state would have a solid Jewish majority with all existing inhabitants remaining in place. That, and not the expulsion of Palestinian Arabs, as Beinart falsely claims, was how the Jewish state was to be established.

Contrary to this Jewish goal of self-determination, even in much reduced territory, the overarching Arab goal was to prevent Jewish sovereignty in any part of the land. This was the goal that animated multiple outbursts of violence against early Jewish Zionist presence in the land, under the Ottomans, and later under the British, as well as the blanket rejection of various partition plans, culminating in the war waged from 1947-1949 by Arabs from all across the region to prevent partition and the establishment of a Jewish state in any borders. It cannot not be emphasised enough that had Arabs accepted any of the partition plans, there would have been two states — one Jewish, one Arab — living side by side in peace and no-one would have been displaced.

If Jews had mimicked the Palestinian version of 'return', which insists on settling in all specific sites where their ancestors had lived, then Jews would have resisted partition again and again, insisting that only the full return to the Temple Mount, Shiloh and Beit El, Hebron and Jericho, and all biblical historical sites where Israel was shaped as a nation, is acceptable and anything less than that is cause for total war. But Zionist Jews were pragmatic enough and realistic enough to understand that to insist on return to the specific places of their ancestors' disregarding changes that occurred on the ground, and ignoring the rights of their neighbors, would mean perpetual war.

In fact, *Palestinian refugees and their descendants had multiple opportunities to mimic the Jewish Zionist version of return into a sovereign state of their own.* Palestinians could have returned to a Palestinian state, that, like the Jewish state, would not encompass each and every place to which they have a historical and emotional connection. This was offered to them by Bill Clinton in 2000 and by Ehud Olmert in 2008. *But Palestinians repeatedly rejected these offers, making it clear that return to an independent sovereign Palestinian state in part of the land was simply not what they wanted.*

Beinart and many others want us to believe that there was once a time when Palestinians supported a two-state solution, but since Israel took steps to prevent it, the only remaining moral choice currently is to settle the Palestinian refugees and their descendants inside Israel. But the two-state solution was never alive, not because of Israeli actions, but due to the Palestinian insistence on settling inside Israel in the name of 'return". This was the reason for the repeated breakdown of multiple rounds of negotiations.

In this effort to paint the dissolution of Jewish sovereignty as a supreme Jewish value, Beinart hopes to shame Jews into becoming willing participants in stripping themselves of their sovereignty by overwhelming them with gruesome details of Israeli actions in the 1948 war. In doing so, he seems to suggest, as many Palestinians do, that supporting their 'return' would be the minimum expected of Jews to atone for their actions in the past. But the horrors of the war itself could not possibly be the reason that Palestinians demand 'return'. If anything, it is the exact reverse. Arab grievance against Zionist Jews predated the war. The war itself was the outcome of the culmination of Arab violent rejection of Zionism that started as soon as the Jews had started building their national home in their ancestral land at the end of the 19th century. The war, the casualties, and the atrocities committed are not the real source of Palestinian grievances: rather, it is losing some of the land — any part of it — to Jewish sovereign control. Palestinian Arabs and Arab armies committed gruesome atrocities throughout the war, which was not necessarily had they only accepted partition. Other conflicts in the world, which took place at the same time, were much bloodier and resulted in many, many more deaths and refugees. Still, no one even imagines Germans returning to the Czech Republic from where they were brutally expelled in 1946, with some hurled into cattle cars with their eyes gouged out as they were sent over the border. Also, no one suggests Pakistanis and Indians returning to their previous homes after the bloody population transfer that took place during the Indian subcontinent's division, when packed train wagons carrying only dead corpses of fleeing refugees crossed the new border.

There is no averting one's eyes from the simple realisation that *the conflict between Jews and Arabs ends and is fully resolved under one of only two stark outcomes: either anti-Zionism renders the Jews no longer in possession of self-determination in the land, as Beinart seems to suggest, or Zionism is finally accepted by the Arab world, and Jewish self-determination is allowed to stand. Short of these two outcomes, the conflict continues, with violence ebbing and flowing and changing forms and means.*

The land between the Jordan River and the Mediterranean Sea can be divided, and so can the water, air, and the natural resources. Security arrangements could be made. Settlements could and have been uprooted. But the thing that could not be reconciled is Zionism with anti-Zionism. Resolution of the conflict, in the sense of it being fully and completely over, means that either Zionism stands, or anti-Zionism stands. Both cannot. There is no 'middle of the road' between Zionism and anti-Zionism. The middle of the road is the conflict we've had for the past 150 years.

Peacemakers must choose which path to peace they favor to resolve the conflict. There are those who seek to end the conflict by ending Zionism, as Beinart does, and so they advocate a wide variety of means for stripping Jews of their sovereignty. Whether they call for 'one state' or 'two states and "return"' or 'justice and rights for Palestinians', these are all formulations that unfortunately still mean that nowhere and in no borders will the Jews govern themselves and exercise power. But we firmly believe that there is yet to appear a viable alternative to Jewish self-determination as a means of securing the safety, dignity and thriving of the Jewish people, and we refuse to be placated by empty promises that Jews would be just fine as a minority living among others, even when there is no more Israel. We do wonder where the people who wave aside concerns about the fate of Jews without sovereignty will be once they are proven wrong. Our path to peace then is that of Arab acceptance of Zionism. Arab acceptance of Zionism is an achievable goal, and the Abraham Accords pointed to what such a future might look like. Yet, it is not likely to become the prevalent position across the Arab world before most Arabs and Palestinians have exhausted all means of ridding the region of the Jewish sovereignty – from wars to terrorism to international condemnation – and found them wanting. This will not happen as long as Palestinian idea of 'return' is indulged by the West.

The West once used to understand a basic truth: that for there to be peace, the war must end. When Palestinians finally come to terms with the fact that their long war against Jewish sovereignty is over and that they can build a future for themselves next to Israel, but not instead of it, there will be peace.

IV.   There Is A Path To Peace, It Is Not Short

CONSTRUCTIVE AMBIGUITY HAS NOT WORKED - PEACE NEEDS CONSTRUCTIVE SPECIFICITY

Essay for Fathom Journal, June 2017

FROM AMBIGUITY TO SPECIFICITY

I am going to reflect on something central to the thinking of many policy-makers working to achieve peace. It is the notion that given the animosity, the distrust and the competing understandings of history, the way to make peace is through 'constructive ambiguity'. Shimon Peres, with whom I had a chance to work for a few years, used to say that 'in love-making, as in with peace-making, you need to close your eyes'. I'm not going to discuss people's preferences in the bedroom, but with respect to peace-making, I think that this perspective is not very helpful. The idea that we can close our eyes a little bit, that we can fudge the issues, that we can use words knowing that we understand those words one way and that the other side understands those same words in a completely different way – I think by now we have enough experience to know that this method is anything but constructive.

We now have two decades of experience with constructive ambiguity and it's clear that we should really call it *destructive* ambiguity. *If we are to move forward what we need is constructive specificity. We need to be very clear about what we mean on the key components, on what makes peace possible and what it means to divide the land between the Jordan River and Mediterranean sea into (to use the words of the UN) 'a Jewish state and an Arab state'. If we are to finally complete the partition, I believe that what is needed is for us to be very specific.*

CONSTRUCTIVE SPECIFICITY ABOUT THE BORDER

What does constructive specificity mean? The first issue is the line of partition. Here we have a lot of words that are being used, such as 'the 1967 lines', 'pre-1967 lines', and in Israel talk of 'settlement blocs' and 'the barrier'. These kinds of words are, in the context of an agreement, used to describe where the border would be. But the time has come to be very specific about what we mean about the line of partition. When we say something like 'the 1967 lines with swaps', it is a good headline but it encourages both sides to continue to be unclear about where that line is. Everyone knows where the pre-1967 lines are, but once we introduce the idea of blocs and swaps it gets muddied.

The one thing that needs to happen, both in Israel and abroad – and this is something I am campaigning for, writing about and proposing that politicians take it as their agenda – is to actually put on the table a very clear delineation of Israel's final eastern border. I have published articles which list the settlements that Israel needs to include within its final eastern border and the ones it needs to exclude. The foreign ministries of Western countries interested in the conflict should do the same thing. Put a map on the table and begin to base a policy on this map. Say 'this is our working map of what we find acceptable'. We know what has undermined both American and EU foreign policy in the eyes of Israelis is that by failing to make a distinction between settlements that will be part of the state of Israel in a future agreement and those which will likely not be, the US and EU have not helped anyone's ability to fully understand what is needed to reach a final agreement.

I propose that the main blocs, except Ariel, should be part of Israel. Ariel goes too deep into the West Bank to be included. I propose that Ma'ale Adumim and Givat Zeev be connected to Israel only with a road. I propose four per cent of the territory of the West Bank, home to about 75 per cent of Israeli settlers, be annexed, with compensating swaps when a peace deal is agreed. Drawing a map would finally end the ambiguity. Once foreign offices in the West have a working map, they can begin to have a policy that is based on this map: much stricter on everything east of this line, but accepting of what is within the line, where building can continue. Policy would become wiser and more credible.

CONSTRUCTIVE SPECIFICITY ABOUT JERUSALEM

The second issue is Jerusalem. People mean different things when they speak of Jerusalem so, again, we need to be very clear. Jerusalem includes:

(a) The Jewish neighbourhoods west of the 1967 lines. Having grown up there I can assure you there is nothing holy or anything to get excited about in that part of Jerusalem. It is time for the world to be very clear that there is no question about the status of this part of Jerusalem. Moving western embassies to this part of Jerusalem should not be a big deal. It is time for the world to end the fiction that Jerusalem is an international protectorate to be governed by the world. It was an idea at the time of partition that, because of the war that followed, was never implemented. The time has come to stop toying with that fiction and to say instead 'we recognise that the Jerusalem West of the 1967 line is Israel'.

(b) The Jewish neighbourhoods built east of the 1967-line surrounding Jerusalem should be part of the map that would be put forward. For me, the Jewish neighbourhoods are part of the four per cent of territory, and 75 per cent of the population, that should be annexed to Israel, done in a way that would be minimalistic.

(c) The Arab villages which were not part of Jordanian East Jerusalem but were annexed to Jerusalem or included into the municipal boundaries after 1968. There is no question in my mind that these areas belong to the future Arab state. Again, the world should be very clear that they do not recognise those areas as part of Israel, or Jerusalem, and that they should not be part of united Jerusalem.

(d) Finally, there is the Old City. When people speak of Jerusalem they immediately think of the Western Wall, Temple Mount and al-Aqsa Mosque. However, that amounts to about 1 sq km; everything I have just discussed is nearly 100 sq km. So, we have to be specific. About the Old City, we need to say that this is the only place where the controversy persists, so the status quo will continue, with an emphasis on ensuring access to the religious places until a decision is made on the final status of that square kilometre. The status of everything else can already be specified, and we would be in a much better position to agree on the status of the Old City if we do not let the ambiguity of that *part* spill over into the *whole*.

CONSTRUCTIVE SPECIFICITY ABOUT REFUGEES

And finally, I want to talk about the issue where I think there is the greatest need to be specific, and that is the refugees and the Right of Return. Amazingly, this is the core issue of the conflict from the Arab perspective, and they are still wedded to the maximalist vision that from the Mediterranean Sea to the Jordan River the state of Palestine will be free. Yet this is the area where the West is most blind. There is a term called 'mansplaining' – where men explain away what women have said because women are incapable of explaining something themselves – so I thought of introducing the idea of 'Westplaining' – the idea that Western countries explain away what Palestinians say. So, when Palestinians say 'we will return to Jaffa' or that they will 'never give up the Right of Return', that it is 'a personal right no leader can ever negotiate', and I have met with numerous Western diplomats whose countries donate to the authority that upholds those ideas, UNRWA, and they say to me 'but the Palestinians know they are not coming back, it's just a negotiating card for future talks'. This is not explaining but Westplaining.

And this is why we need to be very specific. The Palestinians and the Arab world in general, as seen in the Saudi initiative, have come to use terms such as 'just' and 'agreed' to explain the solution to 'the refugee problem'. However, these words are interpreted very differently by Arabs, by the West and by Israel. Regarding the term 'refugee' itself, by no other standard apart from UNRWA's would the five million Palestinians registered as refugees today be considered refugees. 80 per cent live west of the Jordan River and have never been displaced, or they are citizens of Jordan. We have an image of refugees as people who have just escaped from war, or who have lost their homes; we don't think of them as middle-class lawyers living in Ramallah. But this is what many Palestinian refugees are. So the term itself is deeply misleading and needs to be replaced.

The expression 'just and agreed' solution to the refugee problem is understood by many in the West and in Israel to mean that the Arab Palestinians will agree to compromise. But anyone who understands the details knows that if a Palestinian leader accepts the two-state solution and recognises Israel, whilst simultaneously insisting on the demand of return, then the only two-state solution they really support is an Arab state east of the Green Line now, and another Arab state west of the Green Line in the future. It means they have yet to accept the UN Partition Plan of an Arab state and a *Jewish* state. It is important to be specific: when the Arabs say a 'just' solution, they mean return. For them, justice is return. By contrast, the West and Israel think that 'just' means several possible solutions such as citizenship in Jordan, or a home in Canada.

Again, take the notion of 'agreed'. Many people think it means that what Israel does not agree to doesn't happen. But the Palestinian think of 'agreed' completely differently. It means agreeing now to what can be got – for example Israel accepting 5,000 Palestinian refugees a year – while not dropping the demand for return. Palestinians emphasise that return is a personal right and that no leader can negotiate it away. What does this mean? It means that even if something is co-signed in an agreement, the demand will always exist. They can agree on a number today, but no agreement can end the demand for return due to the way that they have construed return.

Here, more than with any other issue, we need to be very specific. Israel and the West need to stop using terms like 'just' and 'agreed'. We have even heard officials like former US Secretary of State John Kerry use the words 'reasonable' and 'realistic'. The West and Israel think of a few thousand Palestinians returning as realistic; the Palestine papers demonstrated that the Arabs think Israel can absorb 2-3 million. The time has come to say: first, there has to be complete renunciation of the collective and individual Palestinian demand of a return west of the 1967 line, just as Israel needs to renounce Jewish return east of that border. It could be said that Israel, as a gesture, might allow 5,000 Palestinians to enter, but the numbers should be clear, and it will not be a right. Second, it needs to be clear that there is no legitimate claim to return. I understand that Palestinians will continue to dream of Palestine from the river to the sea – as some Jews may continue to dream of Judea – but there is a difference between people dreaming and the world supporting those dreams. Today, Jews who dream of Judea find themselves isolated in the world while Palestinians who demand Israel west of the 1967 lines do not. Because of the fudging of the words 'just,' 'agreed,' 'realistic,' and because of the continued financial support of the West to UNRWA, the Palestinians still think that they are supported in their maximalist claims rather than isolated.

CONCLUSION

Peace will be based on the understanding that both the Jews and the Palestinians are peoples indigenous to the land. Both have a serious claim to all of it, but if both insist on the exclusive

WE SHOULD ALL BE ZIONISTS

and superior claim to it, it will be war forever. Peace depends on a clear renunciation by both sides of their exclusive claims, and a new understanding – that the other side's existence means they will only have some of the land. And the 'some' needs to be better defined. Even if both sides continue to have dreams, they need a far better understanding of how isolated they will become when those dreams make peace impossible.

WESTERN STATES FAIL TO UNDERSTAND PALESTINIAN 'RIGHT OF RETURN'

Essay for The Spectator World, May 2020

The issue of Palestinian refugees, and the Arab and Palestinian demand that those refugees be allowed to exercise what they call a 'right of return', attracts scant attention. Neither Israel's leaders nor its public, and certainly not the international community, spend very much time discussing it. This is in stark contrast to other core issues. For example, there is endless discussion of the settlements and the military occupation of the territories, which are indeed important; but the Palestinian refugee issue has barely been subjected to any real strategic discussion. There have been no serious attempts at a resolution, or even efforts to place it on the agenda. The problem, in spite of always being cited as one of the core issues of the conflict, has been essentially hidden from view, relegated to the sidelines, left for some vague future date when all other core issues are resolved.

Yet we discovered that perhaps of all the core issues it is the refugee issue that actually deserves to be front and center. Our research revealed that the Palestinian refugee issue is not just one more issue in the conflict; it is probably the issue. The Palestinian conception of themselves as 'refugees from Palestine', and their demand to exercise a so-called right of return, reflect the Palestinians' most profound beliefs about their relationship with the land and their willingness or lack thereof to share any part of it with Jews. And the UN structural support and Western financial support for these Palestinian beliefs has led to the creation of a permanent and ever-growing population of Palestinian refugees, and what is by now a nearly insurmountable obstacle to peace.

The Palestinian demand to 'return' to what became the sovereign state of Israel in 1948 stands as a testament to the Palestinian rejection of the legitimacy of a state for the Jews in any part of their ancestral homeland. Our research led us to conclude that practically nothing could be understood about the Palestinian position in the peace process and the conflict itself — and no effective steps could be taken toward its resolution — without delving deeply into this issue.

Realizing this, we resolved to research, analyze, and describe this issue from its very beginning in the war of 1948 to the present day. By following key historical figures, unearthing new documents, examining key decision points, and providing analyses, our book raises, and answers, the key questions about this overlooked, yet fundamental, issue. Why are there still Palestinian 'refugees' from a war that ended 70 years ago? Why do the Palestinians insist that each and every Palestinian refugee, for generations into perpetuity, has an individual and in fact 'sacred' right to return to the sovereign state of Israel, de- spite there being no actual legal basis for it? Who and what prevented the Palestinian refugees from being rehabilitated as the Jewish refugees from 1948 were? Was it a lack of interest or money, or were there other, ideological, motives? Is the 'right of return' a real demand or just a Palestinian bargaining chip, which can be bargained away when other demands are met? When Palestinians march for 'return' from Gaza in the direction of Israel, what is it they are actually marching for? What does a 'right of return' mean in the context of a comprehensive peace accord? And if this demand is real, can we move forward and, if so, how?

In answering these questions, we tell a tragic story of Western policy repeatedly shooting itself in the foot and working at cross- purposes. The United Nations Relief and Works Agency (UNRWA), the very agency charged with caring for the original Palestinian refugees in the immediate aftermath of the war, and that has been sustained for decades by Western funding with billions of dollars, has instead become a major obstacle to peace and a vehicle for perpetuating the conflict.

Reaching the conclusion, step by historical step, that *UNRWA is part of the problem, and not part of the solution, we call on the international community to dismantle and replace the agency. To that end, we offer specific policy proposals on how to accomplish this without depriving Palestinians of the social services currently provided by UNRWA.*

The policy of Western donor countries should therefore be to secure alternative providers of services so that UNRWA would be fully phased out. The obvious place to begin is the territory governed by the Palestinian Authority. Currently, the Palestinian Authority provides the same educational and social services as UNRWA and in the same territory. This means that in the same cities in the West Bank, PA and UNRWA schools and hospitals work side by side. The PA's services are presented as a crucial part of a state-building effort, in preparation for peace based on a two-state vision, whereas at the same time and in the same territory UNRWA operates a parallel system that preserves the dream of a 'Palestine from the River to the Sea'. If donor countries are serious about the promotion of peace, it makes no sense to preserve a parallel UNRWA system in the Palestinian Authority.

UNRWA's operations should be merged into those of the Palestinian Authority. Donor states could divert all financial support earmarked for running UNRWA schools and hospitals toward the Palestinian Authority. From a practical perspective and from the perspective of the aid dispensed, nothing would change but the sign on the door. UNRWA schools would become PA schools, but the pupils, teachers, and curricula would remain the same. The same goes for hospitals. The same quantity and quality of aid currently provided by UNRWA would continue, but it would come through the Palestinian Authority. The donor states could continue supporting these services as much as they want, but the funding would go through the Palestinian Authority.

If tensions between Hamas and the PA mean that the Palestinian Authority cannot assume responsibility for the provision of services, donor countries could push for the establishment of a new umbrella organization, or one based on existing organizations, whose only purpose is the rehabilitation of Gaza. All international donations for rehabilitation and local needs could be funneled through this new organization, which would be charged with dealing with the entire population of Gaza and would operate schools and hospitals and dispense other forms of aid without reference to refugees and without refugee status being a determining factor in the provision of its aid.

In Jordan, the path to dismantling UNRWA is the most straightforward. There are 2.2 million registered refugees in Jordan, nearly all of whom are also Jordanian citizens — so not actual refugees, under internationally accepted definitions. Most of them do not even use UNRWA services, and UNRWA's budget for its operations in Jordan is relatively low, compared to the number of refugees it registers there. There is therefore no actual reason for UNRWA to operate in Jordan at all.

In Jordan, however, the path to dismantling UNRWA is also the most sensitive politically, given that the issue of the Palestinian refugees is considered directly related to the stability of the Hashemite regime, a valuable Western ally. On July 21, 1951, King Abdullah of Jordan was assassinated by a Palestinian nationalist from the Husseini clan while visiting the Al-Aqsa mosque in Jerusalem because, among other things, he was willing to make peace with the young state of Israel without demanding return, and even naturalized all the refugees in the West Bank and Jordan toward that end. Given that 70 percent of Jordan's citizens are Palestinians (rather than members of the Bedouin tribes), the Hashemite kingdom has become deeply wary of addressing the Palestinian refugee issue ever since the king's assassination.

It is precisely because of the Jordanian monarchy's desire to preserve its own stability and support, certainly among the kingdom's Palestinian majority, that it sees a need to keep the status of the registered refugees on its soil ambiguous. It is difficult, bordering on impossible, to get a consistent answer from Jordanian officials to the question of how the Jordanian state sees its own citizens. Some say that they are unambiguously Jordanians while others say that they are unambiguously Palestinians, who will one day return west of the Jordan River.

The Jordanian regime sees its ability to entertain both these claims simultaneously as a condition for its own survival. For donor countries, therefore, there is a genuine fear that drawing attention to the status of the Palestinian refugees in Jordan and dismantling UNRWA's operations there would have major consequences for the stability of its regime. But the fact that some political considerations dictate the need to register Palestinians as refugees cannot conceal the basic reality that they are simply not refugees. Moreover, the long-term stability of the region would be served much better by solving the conflict and removing the greatest obstacle to its solution by ending the fiction that there are millions of Palestinian refugees with a right of return to the state of Israel.

As for registered refugees in Syria and Lebanon, a different policy is required. Whereas it is clear that Jordan's citizens are not refugees, and those living in Gaza and the West Bank are living already in the Palestine for which they seek recognition, the refugees registered in Syria and Lebanon are in a different situation.

Syria's approach to the Palestinian refugees has enabled them and their descendants to be integrated with great success over the years into the local economy and to enjoy effective residency status, albeit without official citizenship. Between 1949 and 1956, the Syrian government passed laws specific to Palestinian refugees, granting them civil rights on par with those of Syrian citizens, with the exclusion of the right to vote and the right to citizenship. This process culminated in a 1956 law that stated that Palestinians living in the Syrian Arab Republic are on equal footing with Syrian citizens 'in all the laws and valid regulations regarding the rights of employment, commerce and military service while retaining their original nationality'.

It is worth noting that the civil war in Syria highlighted even further the paradoxes inherent in the unique manner in which Palestinian refugees are classified and treated differently from every other group of refugees in the world. The civil war has forced millions of Syrians, including Palestinian refugees living in Syria, to flee to neighboring countries, including Lebanon and Jordan, where UNRWA has official operations. In those countries, the Syrian citizens are cared for by the UNHCR, which is making efforts to find solutions to end their refugee status, whether by integration in their host countries, resettlement in third countries, or repatriation when the conflict ends and if it becomes possible.

The Palestinian refugees from Syria, however, continue to be registered as refugees from Palestine rather than Syria and cared for by UNRWA rather than UNHCR. This, despite the fact that they were habitually residents in Syria, where they had legal status and had fled their homes due to the Syrian civil war. Whereas UNHCR would happily consider Syrians who fled from Syria and gained citizenship in Germany as no longer refugees, UNRWA would still register them as Palestine refugees.

Lebanon is also a unique situation. Out of all the Arab countries to which the Palestinian refugees fled during the 1948 war, the country in which they were treated the worst is Lebanon. It neither naturalized them like Jordan, nor integrated them economically like Syria.

In reality, Lebanon created a system of extreme state-sanctioned discrimination against the Palestinian refugees. The Palestinian refugees and their descendants in Lebanon have been prohibited from employment in over 20 professions and their ability to enter and exit the country is highly limited. Around half live in refugee camps (a similar rate to Gaza) and many live in dire poverty. It is no coincidence that Lebanon hosts far worse forms of Palestinian extremism than either Syria or Jordan. This is a strong indication that the true moderating force with respect to Palestinian refugees is not UNRWA but naturalization or economic integration.

The policy with respect to the Palestinian refugees in Lebanon should be, as with the refugees from Syria, to transfer responsibility for Palestinian registered refugees from UNRWA in Lebanon to UNHCR, with a view to ending their refugee status by means other than return. Donor countries would transfer the funding that currently goes to UNRWA in Lebanon to UNHCR.

We must also challenge traditional thinking about the role of diplomats and negotiators in extended conflicts. Whereas the traditional view looks at diplomats and negotiators who do the work of peacemaking by shuttling between capitals, and forcing reluctant sides into one room where they are strong-armed into making concessions, *The War of Return* argues that in order to be effective, these diplomats and negotiators must first and foremost correctly analyze the root causes of the conflict, and then work continuously over time to remove the real obstacles that stand in the way of making peace.

Our book demonstrates that in the case of Israel and the Palestinians, decades of shuttling, strong-arming the sides, and endless hours of negotiations came to naught because none of the diplomats or negotiators truly understood and dealt with the root causes of the conflict, choosing instead to turn away and focus on that which appeared easier. If, as the Jewish sages say, we are not expected to complete the task, but neither are we free to avoid it, then diplomats and negotiators must move away from fruitless pursuits of sham peacemaking in favor of the hard work actually required to attain true peace.

Our interest in Israeli-Palestinian and Israeli-Arab peace is not theoretical. We both live and raise families in Israel. Being in a perpetual state of war with the Palestinians and the Arab world means that every day bears the prospect of a loved one being wounded or killed because of the conflict. It means that we raise children knowing that each one will have to join the army and certainly face war and possibly death. Peace for us is not a dinner-table discussion subject but an existential necessity. It is our fervent hope that in writing this book we contribute in a meaningful way to real and lasting peace.

TRUMP'S PEACE PLAN COULD STRENGTHEN ARAB-ISRAELI RELATIONS

Op-Ed for the Jewish Telegraphic Agency, February 2020 (prior to the Abraham Accords)

President Donald Trump's Middle East peace plan will probably not achieve its stated goal of bringing peace between Israel and the Palestinians, but it might just bring about peace between Israel and more of its Arab neighbors. Here's why.

Over the past several years, Israel has become an appealing partner to Arab states for two main reasons. Ever since the revolutions known as the Arab Spring toppled several regimes and undermined and threatened the stability of others, Israel's stability in the region has become ever more apparent.

Moreover, as Arab countries in the Gulf increasingly came to perceive Iran as a threat, Israel's stability, military power and political will to limit Iran's power became ever more attractive to those states.

So behind the scenes, Israel, Saudi Arabia and the Gulf states grew closer, sharing intelligence and cooperating on security to confront Iran. Precarious ties with Jordan and Egypt were further cemented by the joint battle against ISIS and, more long-term, by the discovery and mining of substantial gas reserves on Israel's Mediterranean coast. As all of this cooperation became more visible, these Arab countries had to find a way to do so without appearing to abandon the Palestinian cause altogether.

It is easy to dismiss the concerns of non-democratic regimes and argue that they can pursue their economic and security interests with utter disregard for how the public views them. But this opinion betrays a misunderstanding of the extent to which even non-democratic regimes have to navigate public opinion to ensure their continued survival. In fact, for many decades, the positive sentiment in the Arab world towards the Palestinians and the negative one towards Israel was actually used by many regimes to deflect anger away from their own shortcomings.

The dramatic events of the Arab Spring made it ever more necessary for Arab regimes to remain attuned to public sentiment for their survival, but it also began to change that sentiment, as publics increasingly focused on domestic demands. This means that while empathy for the Palestinian cause remains strong across the Arab world, it is no longer uniform, and in some places it is fraying.

There is growing evidence of decreased willingness to place the Palestinian cause above domestic Arab interests. Voices that in the past would have never been heard in the Arab world now appear on local Arab television and social media, questioning why their countries continue to hitch their wagons to the Palestinians, who are prone to rejecting compromise. In some cases, these voices even express open support for Israel.

In the past, Palestinians could generally count on the Arab countries — not just to openly fight wars for their cause, as they did in 1948 and 1967, but to stand firmly behind them, accepting what the Palestinians accept and rejecting what the Palestinians reject. This is no longer the case.

So although the Palestinians were still able to rally the Arab League — a group of Arab countries, which is already a shadow of its former powerful self — to join in their rejection of Trump's plan, their isolation in the Arab world is growing more apparent.

This is the most important aspect, and the greatest news, to come out of the plan's introduction. Not only does the plan reflect the political preferences of the vast majority of Israel's Jews — with the Likud, Blue and White and Israel Beiteinu parties endorsing the plan — but it has been cautiously welcomed by Saudi Arabia, Egypt, Oman, the United Arab Emirates and Qatar as at least a legitimate basis for negotiations.

It also makes vital regional cooperation more likely to continue and strengthen over time.

Israel, for its part, must endorse and adopt the plan in its entirety if it is to serve as a framework that enables the Gulf countries to pursue ever closer cooperation with Israel. It is crucial that even if Israel ultimately annexes the territory designated for Israel in the plan, it does so while making it clear that the remaining territory, assigned in the plan to a Palestinian state, would not be annexed and will be kept for a future Palestinian state.

It is tempting to ridicule the American president's vision, but the plan does offer the prospect of greater peace and prosperity for those countries in the Arab world who accept that Israel and the sovereign Jews have come back to their ancient homeland to stay.

WHY EVEN THE ISRAELI LEFT EMBRACED TRUMP'S PEACE PLAN

Op-Ed for the British Telegraph, February 2020

Much of the genuine criticism of Donald Trump's "Peace to Prosperity" plan for the Middle East emerges from the assumption that there is another plan to be found; a better, more just and fairer one, to which the Palestinians would say yes, and which would then truly bring about peace. I wish it were so, but sadly there is no evidence for such an assumption.

Like many on the Israeli Left, I would have preferred the US President's plan to provide the Palestinians with more land, greater presence in east Jerusalem (almost all of the city's Arab neighbourhoods, rather than just three of them), more of a say in the holy sites, and greater control over their future borders. However, decades of determined words and actions have made it very clear that the Palestinian leadership will say yes only to plans that bring about the end of Israel as the sovereign state of the Jewish people.

To the Palestinians' credit they have never lied nor wavered about their goal of an Arab Palestine stretching "From the River to the Sea". They have been consistent and persistent in its pursuit, whether by wars and terrorism or by seeking to isolate Israel on the international stage. To that end, they have never backed down from their claim that they possess a "right of return" into the sovereign state of Israel.

Exercising this "right of return" would effectively transform Israel into an Arab Islamic state with a Jewish minority, thereby ending Jewish self-rule. Even when negotiating with Israel over two states, Palestinians have remained adamant that this "right of return" (which is neither a right nor a return) is non-negotiable.

WE SHOULD ALL BE ZIONISTS

When some Palestinians claim to support two states, while rejecting any formulation that would deny them the "right of return", the two states which would actually result are a Palestinian state in the West Bank and Gaza and another Palestinian state to replace Israel.

Westerners who genuinely want to believe that there is a peace plan that allows both a Jewish Israel and an Arab Palestine to live side by side in peace, have sought to square the Palestinians' decades of consistent rejectionism by engaging in a practice I have come to term "westplaining". Westplaining means that when Palestinians say "no", westerners explain it means "maybe", and that while Palestinians may insist that the "right of return" is holy and non-negotiable, in reality they "know" deep down it won't really happen.

What Westplaining has sought to mask is the Palestinian view that if the price of an Arab state of Palestine is that the Jewish people will be allowed to retain their sovereign state and self-rule in another part of the land, whichever part that is, then that is too high a price to pay.

Faced with such choices, whether early in 1937 and 1947 or later in 2000 and 2008, the Palestinians have, to date, considered it far better to keep fighting. President Trump's plan is by no means perfect, but its key virtue has emerged from the simple understanding that there is no plan, short of the end of Zionism, to which the Palestinians would say yes.

This is a painful realisation which for many Left-wing Israelis, like myself, was purchased in decades of dashed hopes watching Palestinian leaders walk away from opportunity after opportunity, and in the blood of families blown to bits by suicide bombers days after Palestinians could have had a state. Yet it is the reason the Trump plan has been embraced by the vast majority of Israel's Jews, Left and Right.

Around the world, including in Britain where it was hailed by

Boris Johnson in the House of Commons, it has been welcomed, too. Even a number of Arab countries have voiced their support for the plan, at the very least as a legitimate basis for renewed negotiations. The UAE, Oman and Bahrain all sent ambassadors to its unveiling. Egypt, Saudi Arabia and others have also backed it. Ever since the Arab Spring and the rise of Iran, these Arab countries have been slowly moving away from decades of virulent anti-Zionism, increasingly assessing Israel as a stable and reliable ally.

The plan of the current administration will bring neither peace nor prosperity for the Palestinians, as they will continue consistently and predictably to say no – but it could just bring greater peace between Israel and the Arab world, who hopefully will come one day to recognise Israel and the sovereign Jews as a legitimate presence in the region.

BIDEN JUST THREW ISRAELI-PALESTINIAN PEACE UNDER THE BUS

Op-Ed for Newsweek, April 2021

The Biden Administration announced last week that it is resuming funding for UNRWA, the UN Relief and Works Agency for Palestine Refugees, allocating $150 Million a year as "a means to advance a negotiated two-state solution." Whatever the Administration's true intentions are, advancing a two-state solution cannot seriously be the goal. *The Administration is consciously choosing to fund an agency that is institutionally committed to ensuring that peace will never be possible.*

UNRWA, under the cover of providing social services to Palestinians, is in effect giving political cover to the dream of undoing Israel by nurturing and legitimizing the demand to settle millions of Palestinians inside Israel, within its pre-1967 lines, in the name of "return."

Unless the Administration is keen to extend the Palestinian conflict with Israel, in the hope that one day Israel shall cease to exist as the sovereign state of the Jewish People, it is unclear why it has made such a disastrous policy choice.

UNRWA is one of the greatest, if not *the* greatest obstacle to peace between Israelis and Palestinians. In contrast with normal international standards, UNRWA has its' own distinct definition for Palestinian refugees, which automatically includes all the descendants of the original refugees from the 1948 and 1967 wars.

Today, the majority of UNRWA refugees worldwide are grandchildren and great-grandchildren of the original refugees. Moreover, the vast majority of them are also citizens of other countries or living within territories governed by Palestinians in Palestine, and so are not actually refugees and in no need of resettlement.

UNRWA's definition inflates the number of those who should properly be considered refugees, 20-100 fold. Only a small share of those registered on UNRWA's rosters—those who still live stateless and discriminated against in Syria and Lebanon—are in need of resettlement. But rather than working to resettle them, UNRWA sustains many of them in perpetual limbo, together with their millions of long-settled brethren, in the elusive promise that they will one day be able to settle within Israel and claim Israel itself, rather than the West Bank and Gaza, as Palestine.

The Trump Administration had it right when it decided to defund UNRWA. And the Biden Administration is making a huge mistake upending that decision. To understand the magnitude of this error, imagine if the U.S. took the position that the entire West Bank is disputed, and then allocated funds towards building West Bank settlements and encouraging settlers to live there, while constantly reminding settlers that by legal "right" the entire West Bank is theirs and only theirs. Imagine if the U.S. refrained from ever saying anything that might be construed as implying that the settlers do not have the full right to settle all across the West Bank, and that someday they might be expected to forgo territory, so as not to anger them or hurt their feelings. Finally, after all that, imagine if the U.S. expressed confidence that when the time comes to settle the territorial dispute with the Palestinians, the settlers would somehow accept and support the need for such compromise.

This would be non-sensical to anyone supporting peace by means of two states. And yet, this is exactly how UNRWA operates, maintaining the fiction that one day, the descendants of refugees will be able to "return" to Israel.

Any U.S. intention to refund UNRWA without demanding deep

structural changes is equally nonsensical to the hypothetical we laid out. There are perfectly rational, humane and effective ways to provide public healthcare and education services to Palestinians without fueling the conflict with Israel—in other words, without UNRWA.

For there to be peace, the war must end. This might sound banal, but it is the most important step on the path to making peace between Palestinians and Israel.

As long as Palestinians are indulged by the West in their belief that the war of 1948 remains an open case and that they can undo their failure in that war to prevent Israel's establishment as a sovereign state for the Jewish people by means of mass "refugee return," there is zero possibility that peace will be achieved. Unless the war is clearly understood to have ended, that Israel is here to stay as the sovereign state of the Jewish people, and that millions of Palestinians are not "refugees" from that war and do not possess a "right" to continue the war through "return," peace will remain elusive, and the conflict will continue.

At a time when the Abraham Accords finally mark acceptance by some Arabs of Israel's belonging and permanence in the region, the Biden administration is refinancing an agency that provides international legitimacy to the Palestinian view that Israel is a temporary and illegitimate creation.

It is hard to imagine a more anti-peace U.S. policy choice.

AMERICAN CONSULATE IN EAST JERUSALEM COULD PRESERVE A TWO-STATE SOLUTION

Op-Ed for The Hill, November 2021

As tensions grow over the Biden administration's decision to reopen the U.S. Consulate in Jerusalem, there is a simple solution that, unusual for this conflict, could be a win-win all around. That solution is to reopen an American consulate located deep in East Jerusalem. This would satisfy the goal of reopening the consulate as a means of re-engaging with the Palestinians. It also sends an important message about America's commitment to preserving a two-state solution, including in Jerusalem. And, if done well, it might be a solution that the Israeli government could swallow — and even embrace.

Carving out a solution to the consulate issue — and for the conflict, in general — requires abandoning decades of constructive ambiguity that has proved to be destructive. It is time to inject some constructive specificity into policymaking, such as acknowledging that the American consulate and the consulates of other countries represent de facto embassies to the Palestinians. The problem is that all these countries maintain these consulates in direct contradiction to their professed policy of supporting a two-state solution to the conflict.

The U.S. is the only country that could point to consistent policymaking in reopening its consulate in East Jerusalem. The reason is that the other countries with consulates in Jerusalem continue to place their embassies to the State of Israel in Tel Aviv — a wonderful city but decidedly not Israel's capital. By maintaining their embassies in Tel Aviv, these countries refuse to recognize Jerusalem as Israel's capital. They maintain the fiction that Jerusalem forms a separate body — a Corpus Separatum — under no one's sovereignty, as proposed by the United Nations General Assembly in its 1947 partition proposal.

Yet these countries pursue an entirely incoherent foreign policy. They profess to support a two-state solution. They call East Jerusalem "Occupied Palestinian Territory." Some of them, such as Sweden, even bilaterally recognize Palestine as an already existing state. But if the eastern part of Jerusalem is Palestinian, then surely the western part — which no one contests and is home to no holy sites — is Israeli.

To have any coherence in pursuit of a two-state solution, the policy of foreign countries toward Jerusalem should be determined either by the 1947 proposal or by 1967, the "Green Line." If it is 1947, neither Israelis nor Palestinians have any claim to Jerusalem. Jerusalem is then not Israel's capital to these countries, but also no part of it is "Occupied Palestinian Territory." It means no country should have consulates, representations or de facto embassies anywhere in Jerusalem. If the 1949 ceasefire guides policy, then the western part is recognized as Israel's capital and all embassies should be moved there, and the eastern part as Occupied Palestinian Territory and de facto embassies to Palestine could be stationed there.

What makes no sense is the policy pursued by most countries, whereby Israel is judged by 1947 and Palestinians by 1967. Most countries deny recognition of Israel's capital in any part of Jerusalem — but they effectively recognize Palestinian claims to the eastern part by positioning de facto embassies to Palestine in Jerusalem.

Only the U.S. could claim to pursue a coherent policy in Jerusalem if it re-opens the consulate, given that it has recognized Jerusalem as Israel's capital and placed its embassy there. The only caveat — and it is a big one — is that the U.S. should absolutely not reopen the consulate in its old Agron Road location, well within west Jerusalem. Reopening a de facto American embassy to Palestine in western Jerusalem would send a terrible message that this part of Jerusalem is somehow contested. That is a view held only by those who want the State of Israel to disappear. No Israeli government, on the left or the right, could consent to such an act. No one truly seeking peace would knowingly pursue it.

In recognizing Jerusalem as Israel's capital, the Trump administration made it clear that this does not mean recognizing the municipal boundaries of Jerusalem and that the final borders of Jerusalem are to be negotiated in a conflict-ending agreement. All genuine supporters of two states understand that a large part of the territory that is East Jerusalem today would be part of the State of Palestine and would form its capital. **East Jerusalem** is a vast territory that consists of approximately 70 square miles of Arab villages annexed to the city in 1968 to surround and buffer the emotionally, historically and religiously significant 1 square mile of the Old City of Jerusalem and its immediate environs. The Jewish people, whether in Israel or around the world, have no emotional connection to the Arab villages that have become East Jerusalem through this massive annexation.

By opening a consulate deep in East Jerusalem in one of the Arab villages that are now city neighborhoods, the U.S. could make a serious, thoughtful contribution to delineating the contours of a two-state solution. It would make it clear that specific borders should be negotiated, and that Palestine should have a capital in the Arab neighborhoods that are within Jerusalem's municipal borders. Of course, the deeper in East Jerusalem the location, the more palatable it would be to the Israeli government. And the U.S. could make this even more agreeable to the Israeli government by calling on other countries to move their embassies from Tel Aviv to Jerusalem.

Reopening the consulate at Agron would undermine these goals. It would bring into question the U.S. recognition of Jerusalem as Israel's capital, because what kind of country opens a de facto embassy to another country in the middle of one country's capital? It would undermine any notion that future borders should be negotiated, because if even non-holy, pre-1967 West Jerusalem is contested, then the issue is not borders but Israel's very existence.

It is a rare thing that, in matters involving Jerusalem and the Israeli-Palestinian conflict, there is a solution that could work for all. Reopening the U.S. Consulate deep in East Jerusalem meets the American goal of re-engaging with the Palestinians and reinforces the contours of the two-state solution. It affords the Israeli government a win by moving the American consulate from its previous location in West Jerusalem to the east and calling on other countries to follow suit by moving their embassies to Jerusalem.

Most importantly, it allows the U.S. to demonstrate policy leadership by highlighting a consistent, logical foreign policy in Jerusalem that truly promotes a two-state solution. Such opportunities for foreign policymaking in the pursuit of peace do not come along often.

ISRAEL'S FINAL BORDER

Essay for Mosaic, June 2020

Israel is near the end of a long journey to set its permanent borders. That's what the annexation debate is really about.

Israel is near the end of a long-term journey to set its final borders. The current discussion about a possible Israeli decision to extend its sovereignty over some territories west of the Jordan River—also known as annexation of parts of the West Bank—should be understood in this context. What's going on now is less about the grand reckoning between competing visions of the Jewish state that some portray it as; it's really more about the setting of Israel's last frontier.

At its birth in 1948, Israel did not have a single settled border, except perhaps with the non-belligerent Mediterranean Sea. Having failed in war to prevent the Jews of the land from attaining independence in the land, Israel's Arab neighbors refused to accept their failure. Rather than peace, the most they were willing to concede was a cease-fire in an ongoing war.

Thus ***the agreements negotiated to end the Arab-Israeli war of 1948 were specifically designated cease-fire agreements, meant to provide the Arab side with an opportunity to regroup in order to resume the war against the young state at a later stage*** (which they attempted and failed to do several times in subsequent years, failing most spectacularly in 1967). After 1949, Israelis proceeded to build their country within those cease-fire lines, but acting as if they were borders did not make them so. Neither does the act of referring to the 1948 cease-fire lines as "pre-1967 borders"; Israel's Arab neighbors did not recognize them as borders.

Israel did not have an internationally recognized border for three decades until, at last, the southern border was finalized in the 1979 peace treaty with Egypt. Attaining its next internationally recognized border, to its east, with Jordan, took another fifteen years. It was in 1988 that Jordan renounced its claims to the territory on the West Bank of the Jordan River; in the context of the Oslo process, Jordan signed a peace agreement with Israel in 1994.

Israel's borders with Egypt and Jordan remain to date its only internationally recognized, bilaterally agreed-upon borders. But it does have some other borders that enjoy some, if lesser legitimacy and recognition. To the north, Israel's border with Lebanon reflects the old line between the British and French Mandates, as well as the 1949 cease-fire line. This ostensible border gained greater international legitimacy in 2000 when Israel ended its eighteen-year war in Lebanon by retreating to this line, and when both sides agreed that the United Nations "Blue Line" as delineated by UN cartographers, would be respected by both sides.

Another retreat, from Gaza in 2005, further contributed to setting Israel's border to the south. Although the Gaza disengagement was conducted unilaterally, Israel did take pains to fully retreat to the lines of the 1949 cease-fire, known as the Green Line. The agreement signed in November 2005 between Israel and the Palestinian Authority (which then ruled Gaza) served to place some additional international legitimacy on this line.

The last border to gain some measure of legitimacy is in the Golan Heights, where, 38 years after Israel's official annexation of the territory in 1981, it was officially recognized as Israeli territory by the U.S. in 2019.

These processes have also ended, for all intents and purposes, the domestic debate within Israel about its borders. The borders with Egypt, Jordan, and Lebanon are settled and are no longer disputed. The Gaza border has nearly the same status; however much some people still resent Israel's removal of the Jewish settlements there, or consider disengagement from Gaza a mistake, there is no constituency for re-occupying it. Likewise, Syria's descent into civil war, the Iranian presence there, and the American recognition of Israel sovereignty have all but ended the Israeli domestic debate about whether to keep the Golan Heights.

All that remains is to finalize, in one way or another, the last unresolved section of Israel's eastern border, the part that was not determined in its peace treaty with Jordan.

The Palestinians have for decades now made it clear that they will not sign a bilateral agreement with Israel to set this border, as they remain committed to an Arab Palestine "from the River to the Sea." Meanwhile, Gaza has been transformed into a Hamas-ruled rocket base. Because of these two factors, certain parameters for setting this final section of the border now enjoy wide agreement within Israel: The Israel Defense Forces will remain the only military power west of the Jordan River; the Palestinians will have some form of self-rule in some part of that territory; and Israel will do its utmost to avoid removing settlers.

The reasons for each element of the consensus just articulated are also easy to understand. For most Israelis, military withdrawal from the West Bank altogether is too great a security risk; annexing the entire territory of the West Bank would bring a mass Palestinian population into the state of Israel, which would endanger Israel's future; and removing settlers *en masse* would provoke social and political turmoil that is simply not worth the exchange for anything less than full and true peace.

The current American peace plan comprehends this Israeli consensus and therefore appeals to the large Israeli center. It establishes the Israel Defense Forces as the only military force west of the Jordan River, it provides a pathway for Palestinians, with limited political self-rule, to establish a state of their own on 70 percent of the territory of the West Bank, and it does not entail the removal of settlements. For most Israelis, this is good enough, especially if it is supported by the U.S. and even provides a basis for further normalization with Arab states.

By effectively placing a ceiling on Israel's settlement project, in the form of an official map that sets aside more territory for the Palestinians than they currently control, the American plan brings Israel one step closer in the long and messy process of determining the last section of its eastern border. While this ceiling is much higher and allows more settlement than some on the left think is wise or desirable, it is much lower and allows much less than what is envisioned by some on the right.

Indeed, there are settlers who believe that the ceiling envisioned in the American plan will actually prove to be a floor, a point of departure for further settlement activity in the future. Defenders of this view believe that the current proposal to extend sovereignty to less than the totality of Area C is wise, even though doing so could mean providing hitherto unheard-of settler legitimacy to the idea a Palestinian state. Why? Because they think Palestinian rejectionism is bound to yield ever more opportunities to extend Israeli sovereignty over even more territory, while in the process ensuring that a Palestinian state will never emerge.

Other settlers are, on the other hand, concerned that this ceiling will actually prove less favorable to their cause, as the settler enclaves it creates inside the Palestinian state will become even less practically tenable to defend than they are today. Mainstream Israelis, this faction of settlers predicts, will therefore increasingly wonder why such isolated enclaves are necessary, and why Israel needs to extend its eastern border by hundreds of kilometers in a winding mess just to include a small number of settlers within its sovereign territory.

Though I suspect that the current range of plans will place

a ceiling on Israel's settlement project, and that over time they will lead to an improved and less winding border as the settlement enclaves become untenable, there is no sure way of knowing right now which dynamic is more likely to play itself out; that lack of clarity is the main reason most Israelis prefer the current status quo and do not understand why they're being troubled by the prospect of annexation at this time.

As Israel moves a little bit closer to finalizing the last section of its eastern border, the process is bound to prove messy. It will not have the neat finality of a bilateral agreement with an established state as it did with Egypt and Jordan. It will not provide the clarity of a strategic retreat to a demarcated line as with Lebanon and Gaza. It will not offer the moral and political simplicity of annexing territory that is of clear strategic value and that lacks a civilian population as it did with the Golan Heights. But it will be an answer to a decades-long question nonetheless.

We should therefore not mistake debates over how best to answer that question for some great moral conflict over the future of Israel. What's happening is neither a descent into one-state apartheid, as some on the left contend; nor is it the beginning of salvation as some of the right argue. We are in the final stretches of a process that establishes the state of Israel as a permanent state in the region with recognized borders. Nothing more, but also nothing less.

UAE'S OLIVE BRANCH

Op-Ed for the British Telegraph, August 2020 (on occasion of announcement of Abraham Accords)

The soon-to-be-signed agreement between Israel and the United Arab Emirates is an Arab first. It is not the first peace deal between Israel and an Arab country. That honour belongs to Egypt. But it is the first that holds the prospect of being and feeling like true peace. Israel has had peace agreements with Egypt and Jordan for several decades now. Egypt since 1979, Jordan since 1994. But it is now clear that these were little more than mutual non-aggression pacts. This is not nothing. The Egyptian and Jordanian militaries together account for the greatest death toll exacted from Israel in multiple wars between 1948 and 1973. Egypt and Jordan have the two longest borders with Israel. These deals are important, but they are a far cry from what one imagines as "peace".

Despite signing these agreements, Egypt and Jordan took every opportunity to make it clear that they have no interest in friendly relations with Israel and nothing beyond security co-operation. There has been no broad-based economic cooperation, no open tourism or cultural exchange. Few Israelis venture into those countries, certainly beyond the Sinai Peninsula, and no Egyptians or Jordanians visit Israel. Worse, Egypt and Jordan, in their desperate intent to signal that they are not Israel's friends, have become their sworn enemies in international forums, spearheading various anti-Israel resolutions. Egypt has been for decades the number one producer and purveyor of hard-core anti-Semitic content to the Arab world.

Israelis had resigned themselves to the fact that their accords with Egypt and Jordan were the best that could be hoped for from an Arab country. Then along comes the UAE, proposing a relationship with an Arab country resembling what we have always imagined peace should be. Not only does it speak of two-way tourism, direct flights, and broad-based open economic and scientific co-operation, the entire tone is one of warmth and appreciation.

Since the announcement, my Twitter feed has filled with Emirati accounts posting the UAE and Israeli flags with hearty wishes of peace and desire for mutual visits. Yes, ongoing relations between the UAE and Israel have been an open secret for some time, and the mutual interests are clear, but the decision to "put a ring on it" matters greatly. The fact that the **UAE is punching a massive hole** through the wall of decades of Arab "anti-normalisation" matters, because it goes to the heart of the Arab-Israeli conflict – the Arab and Islamic view that Israel is a foreign implant in the region that must be ejected. Hence the characterisation of Israel as a "European colonialist" and "Crusader" state established by "foreign invaders".

Normalising relations, rather than an icy peace, is an acknowledgement that not only is Israel here to stay, but it belongs in the region. It might seem a bit much to put all this on the UAE, which is a small country, but it punches well above its weight in the Arab world and beyond. Its towering skyscrapers and ambitious architectural projects, international university campuses, glitzy shopping malls, high-class airlines and space programs, the mere names Dubai and Abu Dhabi have become symbols of a future-facing Arab world. When so many states in the region are disintegrating into bloody dysfunction, the UAE shows what Arab functionality looks like.

The fact that the UAE has chosen open warm broad-based relations with Israel thus places this choice clearly in the realm of the future, relegating those still intent on turning a cold shoulder to Israel to an alliance with the past. Those who continue to oppose "normalisation" with Israel, whether in diplomatic relations or on university campuses, will appear increasingly as curmudgeons attached to historical irrelevance.

ARAB SUCCESS AND NORMALIZATION

Essay for the Harvard Journal of Middle Eastern Politics and Policy, Spring 2022

A few months ago, the following headlines appeared within a short time of each other: "UAE Welcomes Israeli Prime Minister on Official Visit," "Dubai Becomes World's First Paperless Government, Saves Over 336 million Papers," "UAE Named Top Country to Live in for Arab Youth for 10th year." These three headlines are supposedly unrelated. Yet, they tell the most hopeful story to come out of the Middle East in a generation. It is the story of Arab success and the way in which normalization with Israel is now associated with Arab success.

For decades, the story of the Arab Middle East, especially in the West, has been one of failure. Notably, in the wake of 9/11, news stories, government reports and UN papers repeatedly decried the systemic failure of the Arab world. The West argued for the need to address the Arab world's various "deficits" such as a democratic deficit, a human rights deficit, and an economic development deficit. The common thread of these stories was of young people growing up in a hopeless society that offered them no future. One implication was that terrorism was an understandable by-product of such youth despair.

One decade after 9/11, the Arab Spring promised a New Hope. At a time when Facebook was still considered a force for good, Westerners looked on with hope as young people flocked to the main squares of Arab capitals chanting "The People Want the Fall of the Regime." They imagined how these "Facebook Revolutions" would bring freedom, democracy, accountable government, and prosperity to the Arab world. Alarmed warnings by Middle East leaders, including Israeli leaders, that the democratic replacement for secular autocratic leaders was going to be either Islamist fundamentalist rule or chaotic breakdown, were considered the grumpy mumblings of a dying old order.

Those warnings proved prescient. The magnitude of the folly of the US going to wars in the Middle East to repair the region's "democratic deficit" became all too evident. The US then declared a "Pivot to Asia," pursuing a policy of disentangling itself from a region that seemed to offer no prospect of foreign policy success.

Yet, as the US began to reduce its footprint in the region, the Gulf states, which for decades were considered nothing more than Western client states, began to create a homegrown model of Arab success. Realizing that they would not be able to rely on oil and the West forever, local leaders began to forge a vision for their societies that would allow them to thrive even in the absence of direct Western support and unlimited oil. This model of Arab success was marked by a fusion of cultural tradition with technological modernity. It was unapologetically Arab and Muslim while fully pursuing all that modernity had to offer, gleaming skyscrapers, ambitious space programs, and branches of international universities and museums.

While the Gulf model of governance wasn't even remotely democratic, it enjoyed widespread legitimacy among the governed. This legitimacy emerged from being rooted in tradition with effective policies in the service of the people's prosperity. This legitimacy was further cemented by policies that combined traditional rewards for tribal loyalty with meritocracy, expanding the number of women and highly educated people in governance.

Increasing numbers of young Arabs flocked to lucrative jobs in the Gulf and soon noticed the success of this model. An Arab colleague recently told me that for a very long time, even as they were flocking to the Gulf for financial gain, Arabs of Egypt and the Levant snubbed their noses at the "Bedouins of the Gulf." But, he said, they suddenly realized that in the process of helping build the shining cities of the Gulf their own cities have been sidelined. The once great urban centers of Arab leadership and ideological ferment of Cairo, Alexandria, Beirut, and Damascus, have given way to the rising cities of the Gulf. He said that it is now clear that the center of the Arab world – culturally, ideologically, and of course economically - has shifted to the Gulf.

In the process, the Gulf states emerged as models not just of economic success, but of Arab and Islamic identity itself. Against the fundamentalist Islamism of ISIS and the chaos of the once Arab secular states, the Gulf monarchies offered a cultural model of a moderate and tolerant Islam. Throughout the decade-long turmoil of the Arab Spring and its aftermath, the Gulf monarchies, together with the monarchies of Jordan and Morocco, realized that they possessed a unique form of Arab and Islamic legitimacy that was grounded in the lineage of the monarchies themselves. They also realized that their legitimacy, a key to their survival, depended on presenting an alternative to ISIS that was unmistakably Islamic, rather than an imported system, whether democracy or secular autocracy.

The leaders of the Gulf states then, each in their own way, embarked on a process of representing a centrist Islam with special emphasis on tolerance. This Islam was grounded in known moderate interpretations of Islam and was therefore unmistakably Islamic. The tolerance expressed itself in a variety of ways, national and religious, including towards Israel and the Jews. *Normalization with Israel thus became a form of "collateral benefit." It is not that the Gulf states chose to normalize relations with Israel without context and against everything else they were doing. On the contrary, normalization with Israel was part and parcel of this new Arab and Islamic projection of success.*

If the Arab world were divided between Failure and Success, Past and Future, War and Peace, the Gulf states were firmly situating themselves on the side of success, future, and peace. In the vision of Gulf leaders these three ideas were intertwined. Gulf leaders were modeling Arab success. Their model represented the Arab future and peace was part of how they pursued this success and brought about this future.

In the wake of the Abraham Accords, I co-authored an op-ed with two young Emiratis, a woman and a man.[i] They argued that "It is time to dispense with the idea that to be a proud Arab and Muslim one must be anti-Zionist." The thing that was most important for my co-writers to include in the essay was the notion of "waste." They wanted to emphasize the extent to which "the inculcation and dissemination of anti-Zionism in the Arab and Islamic world has resulted in a massive waste of valuable resources". They wanted to underscore that it was not just "wasted human and financial resources and unnecessary suffering", but especially "wasted time." As young Emiratis they already had a sense of themselves belonging to a successful Arab future. It was clear to them that Arab hostility to Israel belonged to a past of failure, of which they were no longer part and for which they had no nostalgia.

These sentiments were echoed beyond the Gulf in a remarkable statement issued by hundreds of Iraqi leaders and activists – Sunni and Shia - that gathered in Erbil in the fall of 2021 to call for full normalization with Israel. Echoing the Gulf vision of tying normalization with Israel with moderate Islam, they emphasized in their declaration that "some of us have faced down ISIS and al-Qaeda on the battlefield," and that "we oppose all extremists."[ii] Harking to the Islamic division between the "House of Islam" and the "House of War," they described the Arab countries as divided between those of peace and those of war. They described Syria, Libya, Lebanon and Yemen as "mired in war" while pointing to the Abraham Accords as representing a hopeful trend of "peace, economic development, and brotherhood". These local Iraqi leaders and activists made it clear that in this binary choice they were very much hoping to situate Iraq in the camp of the future – that of Islamic moderation, peace, normalization and Arab success.

The Erbil declaration also highlights the connection between Arab failure and the rejection of Jews, not just in Israel, but those who once lived for millennia across the Middle East. In the declaration, Iraqis called the mass expulsion of Iraq's Jews "the most infamous act" and have tied it to the country's decline. For Iraq to embark on a path to success, the declaration calls on Iraq to "reconnect with the whole of our diaspora, including these Jews" while rejecting "the hypocrisy in some quarters of Iraq that speaks kindly of Iraqi Jews while denigrating their Israeli citizenship, and the Jewish state, which granted them asylum". The UAE, Bahrain, Morocco and even Egypt, have all demonstrated an understanding of this connection, tying their embrace of Israel with celebration of Jewish life in their midst, present and past.

It is unfortunate that some in the West still find it difficult to let go of their notion of Arab failure, discounting the relevance of the UAE and the Abraham Accords. Some in the West might find it difficult to realize that the world is diversifying its models of successful development and governance. Various countries are moving forward by themselves and for themselves. This is excellent news that points to a possible future of locally grown peace and prosperity. The poll that placed the UAE for ten consecutive years, as the country "Young Arabs Would Most Like to Live in and Have Their Own Country Emulate" did not only compare the UAE to other Arab countries. While 47% of respondents, aged 18 to 24, said they would want to live in the Emirates, only 19% chose the US, 15% Canada, 13% France and 11% Germany, as the top five. This demonstrates that, given a successful local model that is unmistakably Arab, young Arabs far prefer their own model to that of the West.

This is cause for celebration, and for a change, it's coming out of the heart of the Arab and Islamic Middle East.

ZIONISM AND ANTI-ZIONISM COURSE SYLLABUS

(Syllabus of course taught during the 2021 Fall Semester at Georgetown University by Einat Wilf as Goldman Visiting Professor)

Zionism is one of history's most successful revolutions. Yet, since its inception, Zionism faced diplomatic and physical obstacles to implementing its vision as well as intellectual opposition to its very idea, which continued even once the idea of Zionism materialized in the form of the state of Israel.

The course will explore Zionist and anti-Zionist thought in tandem by engaging with original texts and key figures who have shaped the more than century-long debates over Zionism and its opposition. The course will do so by exploring how every type of Zionist thought (political, social, religious) was opposed by a certain brand of anti-Zionism, and reflect on how those various debates about Zionism persist to this day.

Course Materials

The following anthology includes many of the readings for this class and is available at the Georgetown University bookstore:

Troy, Gil (2018). *The Zionist Ideas: Visions for the Jewish Homeland – Then, Now, Tomorrow.* University of Nebraska Press: Lincoln, NE. ISBN9780827612556.

In addition, for those wishing to read about Jewish history prior to the modern era, the following book is recommended, but not required:

Johnson, Paul (1987). *A History of The Jews.* Weidenfeld & Nicolson: London, UK. ISBN 184212479X.

COURSE STRUCTURE
Welcome and Course Introduction: Ideas in History
PAIR I - Politics: Emancipation and Political Zionism
PAIR II - Labor: Communism/Socialism/Bundism and Labor Zionism
PAIR III – Religion, Jewish: Jewish Anti-Zionism and Religious Zionism
PAIR IV – Religion, Christianity: Christian Zionism and Christian anti-Zionism
PAIR V – The Middle East: Islamic and Arab anti-Zionism and the Birth of the State of Israel
Secularism: Soviet, Anti-Imperialist, Left Wing Anti-Zionism

WEEKLY READINGS
(1) Welcome and Course Introduction: Ideas in History

Assigned Reading:

Harari, Yuval Noah. "Sapiens. A Brief History of Humankind/Yuval Noah Harari." (2014). Chapter 2: The Tree of Knowledge.

Ferguson, Niall. *Virtual history: Alternatives and counterfactuals*. Hachette UK, 2008. Introduction.

Extra Viewing/Listening:

Harari, Yuval Noah. *What Explains the Rise of Humans?* TED Talk.

Guiding questions for the reading:

On Yuval Noah Harari: What is intersubjective reality? Why are stories critical to human cooperation? How do stories change over time?

On Niall Fergusson: How do we think about ideas history from our vantage point when we already know that some ideas have won and others have lost? Could we avoid retrospective over-determinism?

Guiding questions for class discussion:

What does it mean to think of Zionism and anti-Zionism as stories? Are we capable of assessing Zionism and anti-Zionism in their historical contexts when we already know about the establishment of the State of Israel? Or about the Holocaust? Or about the end of empires and the birth of nationalism? Or about the failure of Communism?

PAIR I - Politics: Emancipation and Political Zionism (2) - Emancipation

Birnbaum, Pierre, and Ira Katznelson, eds. *Paths of emancipation: Jews, states, and citizenship.* Vol. 293. Princeton University Press, 2014. Chapters 1,3,4 – Emancipation and the Liberal Offer (3-36), Emancipation in Germany (59-93), Jews in France (94-127).

Mendelsohn, Moses. *Jerusalem: Religious Power and Judaism.* Section 3 Fidelity to the Mosaic religion

Clermont–Tonnerre. *Speech on Religious Minorities and Questionable Professions* (23 December 1789)

The Assembly of Jewish Notables, *Answers to Napoleon*

Yehuda Leib Gordon (1863). Poem: "Wake, My People!" (Translated by Hillel Halkin) (PDF)

Extra Viewing/Listening:

Film: Fiddler on the Roof.

Professor Ruth Wisse online course on Sholem Aleichem's Tevye the Dairyman. (Tikvah Fund)

Guiding questions for the reading and for class discussion:

What is the dramatic promise of Emancipation? How does it change the condition of the Jews in Europe? What is the price of Emancipation? What is demanded of the Jews? What is the Jewish response to Emancipation?

(3) - Political Zionism

Roshwald, Aviel. *Ethnic Nationalism and the Fall of Empires: Central Europe, the Middle East and Russia, 1914-23.* Routledge, 2002. "Introduction."

Aberbach, David (2012). *The European Jews, Patriotism and the Liberal State 1789-1939.* Routledge. ISBN 9780203079201. Chapter 9, Love Unrequited: The Failure of Jewish Emancipation 1789-1939.

In *The Zionist Ideas* the sections on Zionism: The Prehistory and Origins of the Zionist Movement (xxxiii-xliii), Leon Pinsker (8-11), Theodor Herzl (11-18), Max Nordau (18-22) and Jacob Klatzin (22-24) and cultural Zionism Ahad Ha'am (106-112), Martin Buber (119-123)

Extra Viewing/Listening:

(The Tikvah Fund Herzl Lecture Series by Daniel Polisar https://tikvahfund.org/course/theodor-herzl-birth-political-zionism/Herzl)

Guiding questions for the reading and for class discussion:

What is the broad historical background for the

emergence of Zionism? What is the ideological background for the emergence of Zionism? What is the Zionist analysis of the failure of emancipation? How is Zionism a response to that perceived failure? How does political Zionism relate to Judaism? How does Zionism relate to ideas about empire, nationalism, freedom and self-determination? What does cultural Zionism assume about elitism, the masses, autonomy, sovereignty and politics? And what is the relationship between Zionism as an intellectual endeavor and antisemitism? Does Zionism need or rely on antisemitism for some of its central ideas?

PAIR II - Labor: Communism/Socialism/Bundism and Labor Zionism (4) Communism/Socialism/Bundism

Luxemburg, Rosa. *The National Question*, Part I The Right of Nations

to Self-Determination. (Marxist.org) Lenin, Vladimir. *Excerpts on the Jews.* (Select paragraphs)

Section on Bund in the Jewish Virtual Library.

Guiding questions for the reading and for class discussion:

What is the appeal of Communism to the Jews? How does Communism relate to nationalism, peoples and self-determination? How does Bundism negotiate the universal promise of Communism with Jewish particularism? How does Bundism relate to autonomy, elitism and sovereignty?

(5) Labor Zionism

In *The Zionist Ideas* the sections on Labor Zionism (37-61).

Shlonsky, Avraham. Toil. A Poem. Guiding questions for

the reading and for class discussion:

What is the appeal of Labor Zionism? How does Labor Zionism bring together the particular and the universal? What is the utopia of Labor Zionism as compared with Communism? What is the role of the land and labor in Labor Zionism? What is the relationship of Labor Zionism to Judaism? Is Labor Zionism utopian or practical? How is Labor Zionism an alternative to Communism and Socialism?

Extra Viewing/Listening:

Inventing Our Life: The Kibbutz Experiment. Film Preview.

PAIR III – Religion, Jewish: Jewish Anti-Zionism and Religious Zionism (6) – Jewish Religious Anti-Zionism

Reinharz, Jehuda. *The Conflict between Zionism and Traditionalism before World War I*. Jewish History.

Grand Rabbi Yoel Teitelbaum, Satmar Rebbe, *Introduction to Sefer VaYoel Moshe*

Magid, Shaul. The Satmar are Anti-Zionist. Should We Care? (Tablet Magazine)

Section on Neturei Karta in the Jewish Virtual Library.

Guiding questions for the reading and for class discussion:

What is the basic conflict between secular Zionism and religious anti-Zionism? What goals do secular Zionism and religious anti-Zionism share? What is the Jewish theological basis for religious anti-Zionism? What are the theological challenges of Zionism to Judaism?

(7) Jewish Religious Zionism

In *The Zionist Ideas* the sections on Religious Zionism: Pioneers (85-101), Ben Zion Meir Chai Uziel (234-236), Zvi Yehuda Hekohen Kook (243-244), Eliezer Berkovits (252-254), Gush Emunim (254-255).

Shemer, Naomi. *Jerusalem of Gold*. A Poem.

Extra Viewing/Listening:

End of the 1967 Six-Day War: (Brithpathe video)

Guiding questions for the reading and class discussion:

How was Jewish religion synthesized with Zionism before 1948, between 1948 and 1967, and after 1967? What role did the Six-Day War play in religious Zionism?

PAIR IV – Religion, Christianity: Christian Zionism and Christian anti-Zionism

(8) – Christian Zionism

Byron, George Gordon. *Oh! Weep for Those*. A Poem. https://www.poetryloverspage.com/poets/byron/oh_weep_for_those.html

British Christian Zionism and George Eliot's Daniel Deronda (In Fathom Journal)

British Christian Zionism: The Work of Laurence Oliphant (In Fathom Journal)

Christian Zionism 101(ICEJ) *Christian Zionism* in Jewish Virtual Library

Extra Viewing/Listening:

Professor Ruth Wisse course on Daniel Deronda (Tivah Fund)

Guiding questions for the reading and class discussion:

What are the theological bases for Christian religious support for Zionism? How does Christian Zionism relate to the cultures in which it exists – especially the British and American? What role if any does antisemitism (or opposition to antisemitism) play in Christian Zionism?

(9) – Christian Theological anti-Zionism

Holland, Tom (2019). *Dominion*. Chapter VII: Exodus and XVII: Religion. Little Brown, London UK. ISBN 9781408706978.

Christian Persecution of Jews over the Centuries in US Holocaust Museum (ushmm org)

Blood Libel in Jewish Virtual Library

On Little Saint Hugh of Lincoln: Jacob Rader Marcus, *The Jew in the Medieval World: A Source Book, 315-1791*, Rev. ed. (Cincinnati: Hebrew Union College Press, 1999). pp. 135-140.

Kairos Document: A Moment of Truth, A Word of Faith, Hope and Love from Heart of Palestinian Suffering (2009). (Kairo Palestine)

Sandford, Michael J. "Is Jesus Palestinian? Palestinian Christian Perspectives on Judaism, Ethnicity and the New Testament." *Holy Land Studies* 13.2 (2014): 123-138.

Guiding questions for the reading and class discussion:

How does Christian theology lead to anti-Zionism? What theological challenges does Zionism pose to Christian theology? What ancient Christian anti-Jewish themes appear in Western anti-Zionism?

PAIR V – The Middle East: Islamic and Arab anti-Zionism and the Birth of the State of Israel

(10) – Arab and Islamic anti-Zionism

Zureik, Constantin. *The Meaning of the Disaster. Beirut: Khayat's College Book Cooperative, 1956.*

The Palestinian Charter

The Charter of Allah: The Platform of the Islamic Resistance Movement (Hamas).

Julius, Lyn (2018). *Uprooted: How 3000 Years of Jewish Civilisation in the Arab World Vanished Overnight.*

The Myth of Peaceful Coexistence 35-44

The Perennial Dhimmi 61

The Legacy of the Nazi Era 79-96

What Came First: Anti-Semitism or Anti-Zionism 119-133

Schwartz, Adi. *The Inconvenient Truth about Jews from Arab Lands.* In Haaretz, May 29, 2014.

In *The Zionist Ideas* the section on Albert Memmi (164-167)

Linfield, Susie. Chapter on *Albert Memmi: Zionism as National Liberation* from The Lion's Den: Zionism and the Left from Hannah Arendt to Noam Chomsky.

Herf, Jeffrey. "Hate Radio The Long, Toxic Afterlife of Nazi Propaganda in the Arab World."

Guiding questions for the reading and class discussion:

What is the status of Jews in Islamic and Arab lands? How is Anti-Zionism related to the history and status of Jews in Arab lands? Is Arab anti-Zionism home grown or imported from the West?

(11) Birth of the State of Israel

In *The Zionist Ideas* the sections on: Israel's Declaration of Independence (145-147) Ze'ev Zabotinsky (67-74)

Oz, Amos. *A Tale of Love and Darkness.* Chapter 44.

Kramer, Martin. *Three Weeks in May: How the Israeli Declaration of Independence Came Together* in Mosaic, May 19, 2021.

Shavit, Ari. My Promised Land. Chapter on Housing Estate, 1957. Basic Law: Israel as the Nation State of the Jewish People.

Extra Viewing/Listening:

UN Partition Deliberation and Vote: YouTube

Declaration of Independence: YouTube

Guiding questions for the reading and class discussion:

What is the relationship between the dream of Zionism and its practice? What does it mean for Israel to be the Jewish state? What does it mean to be a Zionist after 1948? to be an anti-Zionist?

(12) Secularism: Soviet, Anti-Imperialist, Left Wing Anti-Zionism

UNGA Resolution 3379.

Tabarovsky, Isabella. *How Soviet Propaganda informs Contemporary Left Anti-Zionism.* In Tablet June 6, 2019.

Schoenberg, Harris O. "Demonization in Durban: The World Conference Against Racism." *The American Jewish*

Year Book, vol. 102, 2002, pp. 85–111. *JSTOR*,

Anderson, Perry. "The House of Zion." *new Left review* 96 (2015): 5-37.

Mor, Shany. "On Three Anti-Zionisms." *Israel Studies*, vol. 24, no. 2, 2019, pp. 206–216. *JSTOR*,

Extra Viewing/Listening:

UNGA Debate on Resolution 3379 (including Chaim Herzog's speech):

Daniel Patrick Moynihan UNGA speech on Resolution 3379 (five-minute section)

Guiding questions for the reading and class discussion:

What is the relationship between anti-Zionism as an ideology or philosophical worldview and the Palestinian struggle or the larger Arab war against Israel? How are the three separate concepts of *anti-Zionism, criticism of Israel,* and *antisemitism* related? Where do Zionism and anti-Zionism fit into a larger discussion of nationalism, imperialism, liberation, and anti-racism?

The illustration of the cover, by Avraham Vofsi, is based on Einat Wilf's first Labor Party primaries campaign photo with the Half Lira bill of Israel from the 1950's.

ABOUT THE AUTHOR

Dr. Einat Wilf

 Dr. Einat Wilf is a leading thinker on matters of foreign policy, economics, education, Israel and Zionism. She was a member of the Israeli Parliament from 2010-2013, where she served as Chair of the Education Committee and Member of the influential Foreign Affairs and Defense Committee.

Born and raised in Israel, Dr. Wilf served as an Intelligence Officer in the Israel Defense Forces, Foreign Policy Advisor to Vice Prime Minister Shimon Peres and a strategic consultant with McKinsey & Company.

Dr. Wilf has a BA from Harvard, an MBA from INSEAD in France, and a PhD in Political Science from the University of Cambridge. She has has served as the Goldman Visiting Professor at Georgetown University.

BOOKS BY THIS AUTHOR

The War Of Return: How Western Indulgence Of The Palestinian Dream Has Obstructed The Path To Peace

Telling Our Story: Essays On Zionism, The Middle East, And The Path To Peace

Winning The War Of Words: Essays On Zionism And Israel

It's Not The Electoral System, Stupid (In Hebrew)

Back To Basics: How To Save Israeli Education At No Additional Cost (In Hebrew)

My Israel, Our Generation

Made in the USA
Middletown, DE
02 October 2022

11707725R00126